C. Hodgs

(1840-1910)

Durham Architect,

and

his Churches

by

John Wickstead

Durham County Local History Society, 2002

Originated by Peter McConochie, History of Education Project,
The Miners' Hall, Red Hill, Durham, DH1 4BB.
Published by Durham County Local History Society 2002.
Editor: Professor G.R. Batho, tel/fax: 0191 370 9941
e-mail: gordon.batho@btopenworld.com
website : www.btinternet.com/~gordon.batho

CONTENTS

List of Illustrations

INTRODUCTION

Before ordination I had worshipped fairly regularly in two churches designed by C. Hodgson Fowler. Both attracted me as churches and as architecture, and a mild interest was evoked in the shadowy figure behind them. In my first incumbency I had another of Fowler's buildings amongst the churches in my charge. Beyond the barest details of potted biography which are found in the appendices of architectural textbooks, I could find nothing about Hodgson Fowler in print. When later the opportunity came to take a period of three months sabbatical leave, Fowler and his churches seemed a natural choice for a little gentle research. This pamphlet is the result.

There is a vast quantity of historical documentary material relating to the churches, but so far I have been unable to discover any of Fowler's personal papers. My impressions of the man are therefore based on what is published of his architectural and antiquarian papers, and on what others wrote and said of him, chiefly at the time of his death.

It will be appreciated that there is a limit to what may be achieved in three months, especially if a sabbatical is to have some element of 'sabbath' in it. This is therefore a very incomplete and provisional survey, of which parts may be completely inaccurate, and I accept responsibility for any inaccuracies there may be. There remain a large number of avenues of enquiry still untrodden, and many questions still unanswered.

During my sabbatical I was able to visit (or revisit), note, and photograph more than fifty of the churches. In addition, there were others which had previously been visited and photographed. If certain churches, even significant ones, appear to be missing from consideration here, it is either because I was unaware of their existence, or that I could not obtain descriptions of those I was unable to visit before this paper was completed. I hope that this account might stimulate a little more interest in Hodgson Fowler's churches, and perhaps even encourage someone to pursue the subject more expertly and systematically.

Despite its little worth, I therefore dedicate this short survey to the memory of a very significant churchman and architect – Charles Hodgson Fowler M.A., F.S.A., F.R.I.B.A.

John Wickstead, Skegness Rectory, July 2000.

ACKNOWLEDGEMENTS

There are a large number of people to whom I am very grateful. Firstly I express my thanks to my own family, and especially to my wife, Alison. They have had to endure this mild obsession and the inconveniences and absences it has brought. Thanks are particularly due to my daughter, Helen, who has so willingly acted as research assistant for sources in London.

My thanks are due to the Bishop of Lincoln and his staff, who agreed to my taking sabbatical leave, and I am extremely grateful to my parochial colleagues, Fr. Philip Brent and Fr. Jonnie Parkin, who, in accepting the work load of a big and busy parish, enabled me to take study leave without professional anxiety. Thanks are also due to Sam Scorer, F.R.I.B.A., who provided many helpful suggestions in the initial stages of my research.

The Principal of St. Chad's College, Durham, Revd. Dr. Joseph Cassidy, played a very helpful part in making me a Visiting Fellow of the College. (His predecessor, Principal Moulsdale, attended Hodgson Fowler's funeral.) This afforded me a very comfortable base for research in the north east, as well as the stimulating company of a convivial Senior Common Room.

A heartfelt word of thanks must go to all the clergy, churchwardens and other churchpeople, who allowed me access to their churches as well as, so often, giving of their local knowledge and time, in being on hand personally when I visited. (Some even insisted on feeding me!) It was a great pleasure to meet them all. They are too numerous to thank individually, but mention must be made of Canon John Ruscoe of South Hylton who took such a kind interest in my project and pointed me to churches in Co.Durham of which I was unaware.

I have also to thank the archivists, librarians and other helpful staff of the following institutions: Lincoln Central Library, Durham University Library, Tyne and Wear Archives, Durham County Record Office, Lincolnshire Archives, the R.I.B.A. Library, and the Resources Centre of Newcastle-upon-Tyne University Architecture Department.

There are many others who have provided encouragement and important pieces of the jigsaw. I hope they will forgive me if I do not mention all of them.

CHAPTER ONE
The early years and training

Charles Hodgson Fowler was born on St. Chad's Day, 2nd March, 1840, at Southwell in Nottinghamshire. His father was a minor canon of the Collegiate Minster Church, which was later to become a cathedral at the foundation of the Diocese of Southwell in 1884. Charles was the second son of the Revd. Robert Hodgson Fowler and Mrs. Frances Elizabeth Fowler (née Bish.) It was a clerical family. Not only was his father ordained, but so also were his grandfather and brother, and the family had long connections with Southwell. His grandfather, also Charles, had been a chorister there, and after ordination, became a Vicar Choral of Southwell, and later (1802–1840) Vicar of Rolleston, which is between Southwell and Newark. He held other benefices in the gift of the prebends of Southwell (Eaton, Woodborough, and Morton) in plurality until his death on 29th March 1840.[1]

Charles Senior was succeeded at Rolleston by his son, Robert, early in 1841[2], and it was there that Charles Hodgson Fowler spent his infant years. His brother, Robert Rodney, was nearly eleven years older, and carried on the family tradition, being ordained deacon in 1853 and priest in the following year. After eight years as a minor canon of Worcester, he became Rector of Broadway, Worcestershire, where he stayed until he died on 3rd January 1914.[3]

His father died on 2nd January 1858, when Charles was only 17. There has been some speculation that, had his father not died so early, he too may have been ordained. Although he was the first man of his family for three generations not to go to Oxbridge, against this speculation stands the fact that, at the time of his father's death Charles had been a pupil of George Gilbert Scott for more than a year. He therefore probably had shown an inclination and commitment to the architect's profession at an early age.

Charles was educated at Southwell and Berkhamsted Schools and by private tutor.[4] He became a pupil of Scott at the age of 16 in 1856 and served in his office until 1860. Fowler therefore entered Scott's office at roughly the same time as George Frederick Bodley was leaving it, but he was a contemporary there of Thomas Garner, Bodley's future partner. It is interesting that, at least superficially, there are similarities between some of Fowler's work and that of his more illustrious senior. In his early work Bodley eschewed the detailed mouldings, the endless copying of which he had found so tedious in Scott's office, and designed buildings with plain surfaces and simple detail as at St. Martin's Scarborough (1862). In the early churches designed by Hodgson Fowler for the Durham coalfield in the 1860s, there is a similar feel, with the use of plate tracery and Early English detail, as at St. Peter's Harton (South Shields), Leadgate and Tow Law. Later, when Fowler was sufficiently well established to attract more well funded commissions, some of his work again bears a superficial similarity to Bodley's, with an extensive use of late 14th century motifs. (See St. Peter's Norton, Yorkshire, St. Helen's Grove, Nottinghamshire, St. Laurence's Revesby, Lincolnshire, and All Saints, Lincoln)

Also contemporary with Fowler in Scott's office was Robert J. Johnson who was, in 1870, to act as one of Fowler's sponsors when he was proposed for Fellowship of the Royal Institute of British Architects, and who practised in Newcastle only a few miles up the Great North Road from Fowler's practice in Durham. Yet another contemporary was Edward Robert Robson, five years Fowler's senior, and later his predecessor as Clerk of the Works at Durham Cathedral. Other contemporaries included George Gilbert Scott Jun., and John Oldrid Scott.[5]

An interesting account of life in Scott's office in the late 1850s was given by T.G.Jackson, a pupil from 1858 to 1861:

> Scott's office was a very large one. Counting pupils, salaried assistants, and clerks, I think we were twenty seven in all. I was put to work in the first floor room at the back with six others ... Of Scott we saw but little. He was up to the eyes in engagements and it was hard to get him to look at our work. I have seen three or four men with drawings requiring correction or approval grouped outside his door. The door flew open and out he came. 'No time today!', the cab was at the door and he whirled away to some cathedral where he would spend a couple of hours and then fly off again to some other great work at the other end of the kingdom ... It need hardly be said that it is an impossibility really to direct so large a staff as Scott's but the work had to be done somehow. The heads of different rooms were capable men with a good knowledge of construction; Scott had a wonderful power of making rapid expressive sketches and from these his men were able to produce work which, curiously enough, did fall into something of a consistent style that passed for Gilbert Scott's ...[6]

Fowler's practice was, of course, not as extensive or prestigious as Scott's, but in the last three decades of his life, the impression is given by his notebooks and by the amount of work being produced by his office that he was a man who was almost equally busy and active. Like Scott, Fowler seems to have produced sketches which were worked up by his assistants – men like G.W. Footit, H. Cayley and G.W. Milburn.

More than one hundred pupils and assistants passed through Scott's office, and its effect on the architecture of late 19th century Britain was considerable. During the years Fowler was a pupil, Scott was concerned with broadening the base of his practice and to make a name in the designing of great public buildings and country houses. In late 1857 John Murray published Scott's book on secular Gothic architecture, *Remarks on Secular and Domestic Architecture Present and Future.* In this Scott argued that domestic architecture was in a parlous state, and that a reformation could be effected by ending the unnatural division between secular and church architecture. He advocated Gothic as the adaptable style through which such a transformation could be brought about.

In 1855 Scott had designed a Town Hall for the city of Hamburg, a project which came to nought when the city fathers diverted the capital to the improvement of the city's canals. Similarly designs in 1856 for new Town Halls at Halifax and Bradford were not executed. In 1858 however Scott began the building of Kelham Hall, a Gothic pile on the banks of the Trent not far from Fowler's boyhood home at Rolleston. This building later was to become well-known in the Church of England as the home of the Society of the Sacred Mission and its theological college. It is now the headquarters of Newark District Council.

In 1856 Scott entered the competition to design the new Foreign Office building There were 210 entries of which only 10 were Gothic in style, one being Scott's. He was placed third. Lengthy parliamentary machinations ensued and Scott became involved in a heated Gothic versus Classical battle. In the end, although he was commissioned, he was forced to prepare a classical design which Sir Reginald Blomfield later described as, 'one of the most boring buildings in London.'[7]

Such was part of the background to Fowler's training. Happily during this period the ecclesiastical work of Scott's office also continued apace, and presumably it is that with which Fowler would have been most familiar. In 1855 the lengthy project for the restoration of Lichfield Cathedral had begun, and in the late 1850s there was an increase in the number of church restorations undertaken. Amongst these were Holy Trinity Coventry, Oakham and Crowland Abbey.

Perhaps Scott's best known new work of this period is the chapel of Exeter College, Oxford (1858–9), a design based on St. Chapelle, Paris. This obviously had little influence on Fowler for he eschewed all things French. Three major new projects of this period do however display features which were to appear in Fowler's own early work.[8] St. Matthias' Richmond, Surrey, of 1857–8 is a high pitched church with late 13th century details and a wheel window at the west end. Hodgson Fowler's early churches all have late 13th century detail, and wheel windows feature at the west end at Harton (South Shields), Leadgate and, very prominently, at Tow Law. The churches designed by Scott for Leafield, Oxfordshire, and Ranmore, Surrey, also have 13th century details and both have towers with octagonal upper stages and spires. The latter is a striking feature of Fowler's early church at Harton.

In the R.I.B.A. Drawings Collection there are two sets of drawings from this period of Hodgson Fowler's life. They are of St. Peter's church, Preston, Surrey and are dated 1860.[9] Fowler probably left Scott's office that year at the age of twenty. In 1862 he exhibited a picture at the Royal Academy Summer Exhibition entitled, 'In the Rue des Aguilles, Bruges.'[10] This might suggest that some of the time before he was elected A.R.I.B.A. in 1863 was spent abroad.

Charles Hodgson Fowler was proposed for Associateship of the R.I.B.A. on 22nd October 1863. The illustrious Fellows of the Institute who proposed and recommended the young man were George Gilbert Scott, E. Welby Pugin and M. Digby Wyatt – a trio of some weight. The proposal was approved by the R.I.B.A. Council on 26th October and Fowler was elected A.R.I.B.A. on 30th November, signing the necessary declaration on 4th December.[11]

Hodgson Fowler's address at this time is given as 4 St. George's Road, Eccleston Square, Pimlico. This was close to the newly opened Victoria Station which had been built on the site of the basin of the Grosvenor Canal in 1860. The canal itself, now narrowed, still existed next door but one to Fowler's home, but it disappeared, as presumably did No. 4 St. George's Road, when the railway was widened in 1902.[12] The houses now begin at No.8 and the road has been renamed St. George's Drive.

CHAPTER TWO
The Professional Architect

Early Practice

Hodgson Fowler's professional potential seems to have been highly esteemed, for on 24th September 1864, at the age of only 24, he was appointed Clerk of the Works at Durham Cathedral in succession to his older contemporary in Scott's office, E.R. Robson.[1] This appointment laid the foundation for a practice in Durham which was to grow, develop and last until Fowler's death 46 years later. The professional connection with the Cathedral was also to last for the rest of his life.

Almost immediately Fowler began designing new churches in his own right. It speaks highly of the regard in which he was held that such commissions were entrusted to a young man in his mid-twenties. From this period date designs for churches at St. Ives, Leadgate near Consett, St. Peter's, Harton in South Shields, St. Cuthbert's East Rainton, St. Paul's Haswell, St. Andrew's Howden-le-Wear, and Ss. Philip and James Tow Law.[2]

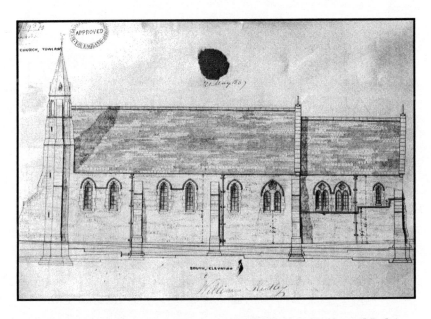

Fowler's own drawing for Tow Law south elevation (Durham C.R.O.)

11

To someone familiar with the style of Fowler's later work further south these churches are rather surprising. They have features which he denigrated in papers delivered a decade or so later. They possibly show the influence of his training and echo the work of an earlier generation. They have much 13th century detail. Lancets, singly and in groups, abound, and there is much use of plate tracery, stiff leaf and wheel windows.

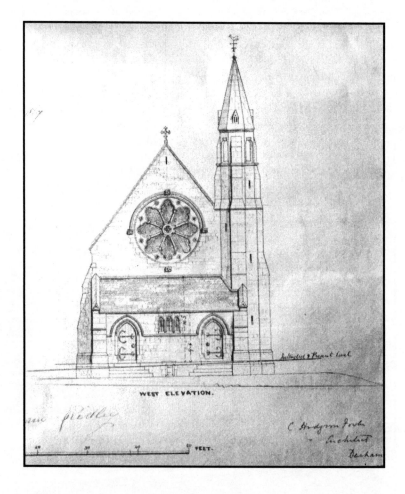

Fowler's own drawing for Tow Law west elevation (Durham C.R.O.)

Of these early churches perhaps the most successful are at Leadgate and Tow Law. St. Ives Leadgate is a big rather plain stone church. A high pitched nave of five bays has arcades with round pillars, square abaci, and plain unchamfered arches, above which there is a clerestory of plate traceried round windows. There are low aisles (the north added later in 1879), and a wheel window of plate tracery above two lancets at the west end. The church at Tow Law is better. It is a simple stone church of spacious nave and chancel with organ chamber and vestry to the north. There is a long low porch (almost like a narthex) against the west wall, and an octagonal spirelet at the north west corner. Again the roofs are high pitched, and there is plate tracery in the chancel with lancets in the nave. The large wheel window in the west wall is impressive. Despite the interior being spoiled by a later 'folksy' chancel screen constructed from fir cones (!), the overall effect is pleasing and, because of its composition and proportions, more recognisably the work of its architect. It also displays features common in Fowler's later work – small cusped gables at the lower ends of gable copings, and a chancel arch resting on corbels which extend downwards into truncated pilasters or engaged columns. Pevsner describes this church as having, '… a sensitive handling of materials and style characteristic of his work.'[3]

Less successful is St. Peter's Harton at South Shields. It is a rock-faced building, again with plate tracery and, as at Leadgate, two lancets and a wheel at the west end. The most interesting, but slightly strange, feature is a tower at the north west corner which has an octagonal upper storey with a short stumpy spire and a vaulted entrance porch beneath. The effect is not well balanced, and the interior has been ruined by the recent application of a glossy paint scheme in white, grey/brown and blue.

Some references describe the now demolished church of The Holy Innocents at Tudhoe as being by Hodgson Fowler, and perhaps his earliest work (1864)[4], but the drawings in Durham County Record Office, although in the Hodgson Fowler collection, are clearly by E.R. Robson. They have imposed on them pencil sketches by Fowler for later proposed alterations and extensions. It is possible that, like some work at Durham Cathedral, this was a project which Fowler inherited from Robson and supervised. In his early notebooks there are references to work at Tudhoe and the sketch of a font.[5] The basic design was, however, by Robson.

As well as designing new churches as soon as he moved to Durham, Fowler immediately became involved in restoration work and making additions to local churches. In 1864 an organ chamber and vestry was added to St. Oswald's Durham (extended some twenty years later.) In 1865 he was responsible for the reroofing of the nave and aisles of St. Hilda's Hartlepool.

In the same year he was making drawings for proposed additions to Cockfield Church. The earliest of his notebooks contain many sketches and measurements, dated October and November 1865, for work at Cockfield.[6]

Another of his notebooks from the following year gives his address at this time as 5 North Bailey, Durham, a building now occupied by a solicitors' practice. Later Fowler worked from 47 North Bailey and lived very close by in what is now known as No. 16 The College.

Fowler of Durham

Fowler left his mark on both the cathedral and the wider city.

At the Cathedral he inherited work already begun by E.R. Robson. In 1866 he was responsible for the restoration of the north side of the Galilee to Robson's design.[7] Also in the 1860s the medieval gateway to The College (Durham's Cathedral Close), with St. Helen's chapel over it, was restored.[8]

In the 1870s Fowler's former master, Sir Gilbert Scott, undertook a major restoration of the Cathedral, and Fowler should perhaps be credited with more of this work than he normally has been. There are drawings in the Durham Dean and Chapter Muniments of the reordering of the choir, organ, stalls etc., and details of work on the Nine Altars Chapel. Fowler was responsible for the organ case and probably for the rearrangement of the stalls in the choir. He did not approve of the way in which the lancets of the Nine Altars Chapel had been 'tidied up' by the removal of the remaining 15th century tracery. In this Fowler was a much more conservative restorer than Scott, with whom he had also disagreed over the removal of tracery from the west front lancet windows at Ripon.[9]

There was considerable controversy in Durham over the desirability of replacing Cosin's choir screen, which had been removed as recently as the 1840s. Scott eventually provided a work of alabaster, marble and mosaic which, unlike the old screen, allowed a view from the nave down the choir to the east end. Some regarded it as aesthetically perfect, and others thought it hideous, and some still do. What Fowler thought of the controversy and of Scott's design is unknown. There is however in the Dean and Chapter Muniments a drawing showing an alternative design for a choir screen by Hodgson Fowler himself. To those familiar with his later work its design is recognisably his – a wooden screen with some wrought iron detail, richly traceried in late 14th century style.

In the late 1870s Fowler undertook the restoration of the western towers and gable of the Cathedral. He was also responsible for furnishing the Gregory Chapel in the north transept. Later in the 1890s and early 1900s the Slype and Song School rooms over it were renewed to his designs. The monument to Joseph Barber Lightfoot, Bishop of Durham 1879-89, on the north side of the choir is also his work. What Fowler regarded as his 'magnum opus' at the cathedral was his rebuilding of the Chapter House. In 1874 the original east end of the Chapter House, demolished in the 18th century, had been excavated, and Fowler had provided plans of the foundations uncovered. These were published in *Archaeologia* to illustrate a paper delivered on 15th April 1875 by the north east's leading antiquarian, Revd. J.T. Fowler (no relation.)[10] Later, in the early 1890s, Fowler rebuilt the Chapter House on its original foundations at a cost of some £5,000.

In the Dean and Chapter Muniments there are drawings for a proposed new Revestry. Like the choir screen these were never implemented. There are also fascinating designs for such small details as curtain brackets and gas standards. Having been Clerk of the Works for twenty years, in 1885 Hodgson Fowler was officially appointed architect to the Dean and Chapter[11], and in the same year he was awarded an Honorary M.A. by the University of Durham.

Fowler's mark on the city of Durham was by no means restricted to the Cathedral.[12] As well as the work already noted at St. Oswald's church, between 1877 and 1880, he carried out an extensive programme of restoration and additions at St Margaret's church. The few who have heard of C.Hodgson Fowler will naturally associate him with ecclesiastical work, and this did indeed form the bulk of his work. But church commissions were by no means the only work he undertook, and this fact is reflected in Durham city and its environs. In the early years of his career (1868–1870) he prepared plans for Henderson's Carpet Factory, and towards the end of his career he designed the new Gas Company offices on Claypath. This building still stands, although it is spoilt on the ground floor by the insertion of a modern shop front for the Northern Echo newspaper. The Durham County Record Office also has in its extensive Hodgson Fowler collection, drawings for alterations to the Town Hall, a new school for Gilesgate Infants (1883), additions and alterations to St. Oswald's School (1886 & 1891), enlargements and additions to Bede College (1892–3 & 1906), additions to Durham County Hospital (1884–7), and alterations to St. Oswald's Vicarage. In addition to all of this he carried out work at Durham Castle (University College) including the restoration of the chapel where he designed a reredos, altar and other furnishings (1877.)

Fowler made himself a man of Durham in other ways than professionally. He was deeply involved in ecclesiastical politics and he was

15

a keen Volunteer soldier in the 4th (later 8th) battalion, Durham Light Infantry. He retired with the rank of Major and was proud of the Volunteer Decoration bestowed on him by Queen Victoria.[13]

The Mature Professional

On 21st March 1870 Charles Hodgson Fowler was proposed for Fellowship of the R.I.B.A. His sponsors this time were George Gilbert Scott, E. Welby Pugin and Robert Johnson. The proposal was approved by the Council on 28th March, and he was elected F.R.I.B.A. on 16th May.[14]

By the age of 30 Hodgson Fowler had designed seven new churches, of which all but the church attributed to him at Sykehouse in Yorkshire were in County Durham. Indeed, with that one exception, he does not appear to have designed any complete church outside Durham County until the early 1880s when he was in his forties. In the first half of the 1870s Fowler was deeply involved in the restoration work at Durham Cathedral. In the late 1870s his work outside the Cathedral began to increase, and the numbers of churches to which he made additions and for which he prepared schemes of restoration grew. His services also began to be in demand further south.

With the exception of a cemetery chapel for Houghton-le-Spring in 1875, Fowler does not seem to have designed a new church after Tow Law in 1869 until those at Bearpark, Murton, Middleton-in-Teesdale and South Hylton in the late 1870s. But then in the 1880s his career took off. In the last thirty years of his life Fowler was responsible for hundreds of schemes of restoration and additions to churches mainly in Co. Durham, Yorkshire, Lincolnshire and Nottinghamshire. In addition, during the same period, he designed at least fifty new churches, mission churches or chapels.

In several ways the early 1880s mark a watershed in the life and career of Charles Hodgson Fowler. At the age of forty, on 14th September 1880, he was married to Grace Florence Hood, the only daughter of Revd. Frankland Hood of Nettleham Hall near Lincoln.[15] It was the beginning of a decade in which his professional reputation spread geographically, and from the 1880s until his death in 1910 the practice was consistently busy. The 1880s also mark a change in his architectural style to something more mature and recognisably individual. It is interesting that, with one traceable exception[16], all Fowler's work in Lincolnshire follows his marriage into the county's squirearchy. By 1882 he was working on plans for changes and additions to the church at Sausthorpe near Spilsby, where the squires were the Swans, another family connected to his wife's by marriage.[17]

In addition to his appointment at Durham, Fowler was appointed architect to Rochester Cathedral in succession to J.L. Pearson in 1898. At Rochester the central tower was rebuilt under his supervision (1904–05), and he designed the altar tomb of Dean Hole. In 1900 he was also appointed architect to Lincoln Cathedral, where he began a radical rebuilding of the north east corner of the cloister range.[18] Other professional appointments included Diocesan Architect to the dioceses of Durham and York, Hon. Consulting Architect to the Incorporated Society for Promoting the Enlargement, Building and Reparation of Churches and Chapels, Hon. Architect to the Durham Diocesan Church Building Society, and Hon. Architect under the Ecclesiastical Dilapidations Act.

Although at the time of his death he was in negotiations to take W.H. Wood of Newcastle into partnership, Hodgson Fowler continued in professional harness until his unexpected brief final illness. The final notes in his last sketchbook are of dimensions taken at Rochester on the very day he was taken ill.[19] As his obituary in the *Durham County Advertiser* says of him, 'He rapidly attained to a proud position and highly adorned the profession of which he was so renowned a member.'[20]

The Antiquarian and Ecclesiologist

Although C.Hodgson Fowler had not been to university, his contemporaries spoke of him as having, 'a scholarship of no mean order,'[21] of being, 'impressed by his erudition.'[22] and of, 'his distinction as an ecclesiologist.'[23] Like other Victorian architects, Fowler had a deep interest in, and understanding of, things antiquarian and ecclesiological. Indeed he declared the architect's task impossible without such knowledge.

He became a member of the Yorkshire Architectural Society in 1872, becoming a committee member in 1875. He was also a member of the Yorkshire Archaeological and Topographical Association, the Archaeological and Architectural Society of Durham and Northumberland, and the Lincoln and Nottingham Architectural and Archaeological Society. The proceedings and journals of these societies contain papers delivered by Fowler and other contributions which show the depth of his knowledge, and also throw interesting light on his ecclesiological preferences. The young Clerk of the Works at Durham Cathedral while still in his twenties contributed a description of Hamsterley church to the *Transactions of the Durham and*

Northumberland Society. This piece demonstrates an eye for detail and a dislike of 'more modern alterations.'[24] At a meeting of the same society held on 29th May 1872 at Kelloe, Fowler directed the members' attention to the main points of interest about the church and declared, 'it has been deplorably maltreated and scarcely any characteristic old work is left.' The same volume of the Society's Transactions also has a piece by Fowler on desk ends in the chapel of Durham Castle. This paper talks of the recent reparation of the chapel (his work,) and displays a knowledge of heraldry.[25] In the late 1900s the *Transactions* of the Society speak of excavations of the cloister at Durham being allowed under Fowler's superintendence.

The *Yorkshire Archaeological Journal* noted in 1886 that the Council of the Yorkshire Archaeological and Topographical Association were concerned about the dangerous state of the west front at the ruined church of Byland Abbey. They were very glad to find that the owner had already contacted Hodgson Fowler, and they felt, 'sure that the ruins of this beautiful Abbey could not be in more reverent or more skilful hands.' They printed Fowler's report and suggestions for reparation. The owner's agent reported on various items discovered when the rubbish was cleared and how the work had been carried out as Fowler had instructed.[26] Hodgson Fowler the antiquarian and architect was also called in to give advice on ruins in his home county. *The Newark Advertiser* in an article on the renovation of Newark Castle speaks of 'Mr. Hodgson Fowler, the well-known architect,' who was consulted about its repair[27], and an entry in the ledger of Newark U.D.C. Castle Gardens Committee records a payment to Fowler of £11 2s 0d as his commission in connection with the castle restoration.

Papers delivered to the Yorkshire, and Lincoln and Nottingham Architectural Societies were published in the Associated Architectural Societies Reports and Papers. The 1877 volume includes illustrated papers on Glentworth church (Lincs.), where Fowler described the 1782 nave as hideous, and Stillingfleet church (Yorks.), where he carried out an extensive restoration scheme.[28] The 1880 volume includes an illustrated account of Salton church (Yorks.), which Fowler also restored, and a significant paper on, 'Some Characteristics of Nottinghamshire Churches,'.[29] Another important and enlightening paper, delivered to the Lincoln and Nottingham Society, was published in the 1883 volume under the title, 'Church Restoration : What to do, and what to avoid.'[30]

On 6th June 1878 Hodgson Fowler was elected a Fellow of the Society of Antiquaries of London. Although he does not appear to have played a great part in the Society's activities, this Fellowship seems to have had considerable significance for him, for from this time onwards he invariably signed architectural drawings and plans as, 'C.Hodgson Fowler F.S.A.' *Archaeologia*, the Society's journal published Revd. J.T. Fowler's paper on the excavations of Durham Chapter House complete with Hodgson Fowler's plans.[31] In the Society's *Proceedings* for 22nd January 1880 an account is given of Fowler exhibiting a ring found at Southwell Minster on the hand of a skeleton thought to be that of Laurence Booth, Archbishop of York (ob. 1480), and in the *Proceedings* for 23rd May 1889 there is a note of Fowler's about a 13th century grave slab discovered during the rebuilding of Easington church in the North Riding of Yorkshire.

When interesting carved stones were found during Fowler's rebuilding or restoration of a church, he made a practice of displaying them in the new walls. This was done, for example, at South Kyme (Lincs.), and there are very interesting pieces of Saxon work in the walls of the rebuilt church at High Hoyland (Yorks.)

The Drawings, Notebooks and Documents

Unfortunately it has not been possible so far to locate any personal papers, but it is appropriate to make a brief note about the large quantity of documents left behind by Fowler's long professional practice.

After Fowler's comparatively sudden death, William H. Wood took over the practice completely and by 1912 the whole business had moved to Newcastle. In 1927 Wood took a partner, Edmund Oakley, and it was the documents of Wood and Oakley, including those inherited from C. Hodgson Fowler, which eventually found their way to Newcastle City Archives (now Tyne and Wear Archive.) Sadly but understandably the collection was split, and the drawings and plans have been distributed to the relevant record offices all over the country.

Tyne and Wear Archive retain 95 of Fowler's notebooks and sketchbooks dating from 1865 to 1910. They are all small pocket books. The contents sometimes seem chaotic, and they are not always used in chronological sequence. Some have been started at one end and then later turned around and restarted from the other. The earlier volumes are superficially more interesting, for in his twenties, Fowler jotted down or sketched whatever seemed to take his fancy. The very first, as well as containing sketches and notes for work under way at Cockfield, Tudhoe, Harton and East Rainton, contains ephemera like a sketch of a bracket at Barnard Castle Railway Station, a Windsor chair, and an intriguing note that Johnston Hogg of Pilgrim Street, Newcastle, charge $3/4\%$.[32] A notebook dated 1869 has a charming sketch of the Vicarage and church in his home village of Rolleston.

Later volumes are more business-like with numerous measurements and mouldings. But there are also drafts of letters to clergy, and instructions to masons, builders and joiners (presumably for Bills of Quantity.) Volumes from the 1880s contain sketches of what were to become the churches at Beadlam and Great Habton in Yorkshire. The most poignant entry is the last in Fowler's hand – faint and shaky measurements made at Rochester and dated 2nd December 1910, the day on which Fowler was taken with his final illness.

These notebooks and sketchbooks would repay detailed and lengthy examination before following them up in the drawings and on the ground. The drawings from Fowler's office are not of the pretty kind which might make them sought after for decorating middle class hallways and studies, but they are executed with a clear crisp draughtsmanship, and sometimes illustrate the process involved in the design of a new church or addition. For example, the drawings held in Lincolnshire Archives indicate that at one time a very different building was planned for St. Faith's Lincoln than that finally erected. There are drawings showing a much taller building with a clerestory – not unlike the church built in the following decade on the other side of the city at All Saints. At some point a tower seems also to have been envisaged but not proceeded with.

Most of the drawings appear to be kept in the record offices in the state in which they were received from the firm's office – rolled in bundles tied with tape. When unrolled, unless handled very carefully, they are prone to crack and tear. Some are in a very poor condition. Because the buildings to which they refer are unfashionable their inspection is probably rarely requested. It is understandable therefore that it is difficult for hard-pressed archives to find the resources for their conservation.

A good argument therefore might be made for reassembling all the drawings, notebooks and papers in one central Hodgson Fowler archive, perhaps at Durham, Newcastle or even the R.I.B.A. This might more readily generate funds for conservation, and more easily facilitate study in depth. Incumbents and Parochial Church Councils might also be more ready to hand over documents and plans they retain to a central Fowler archive of higher profile.

CHAPTER THREE
Restoration, reparation and additions

The greatest part of Fowler's work numerically was in restoring, rebuilding and making additions to existing church buildings. His approach to restoration is illuminated by the paper he delivered to the Lincoln Diocesan Architectural Society, 'Church Restoration: What to do, and what to avoid.'[1] Instead of talking of 'restoration' Hodgson Fowler preferred the term 'reparation' which he defined as, '... the act of repairing a fabric, or putting it into good order and soundness of construction.' 'Restoration', on the other hand, implied the alteration of the fabric into what it might have been in its original state, 'or rather to the idea of its original state, found in the brain of the architect.' The latter, he argued, had done untold harm and had led to the most deplorable results. He gave as an example the way in which fine clerestories had been swept away to be replaced by new high-pitched roofs. It is interesting to note that this is what had been done by Ewan Christian in his 1870 restoration of the church at Sturton-le-Steeple, Nottinghamshire. After a disastrous fire in 1901, Fowler replaced the clerestory when he rebuilt the church.[2] Fowler also decried the way in which, in the name of restoring things to their original state, fine Decorated and Perpendicular windows had been removed to be replaced by lancets or even mock-Norman windows as had happened at Southwell Minster.

Fowler advocated an approach to church restoration which, in modern terms, might be termed 'integrated.' For proper reparation it was an absolute necessity for the architect to possess a knowledge of ecclesiological and antiquarian matters, not just in the field of architecture, but also in painting, sculpture, music, stained glass, embroidery, ritual and ecclesiastical history. That he personally possessed this knowledge is demonstrated in the churches he built. Moreover Fowler's own work cannot be properly appreciated without some understanding of his Tractarian churchmanship, and, in relation to restoration, he argued that a knowledge of medieval ritual was absolutely necessary if the many things we come across in our old churches are to be understood. He also insisted that not only a deep knowledge of architecture in general was required, but also a knowledge of the local style and how it varies from the rest of the country. The Decorated and Perpendicular styles are not the same in Yorkshire as in the south, but are full of local peculiarities.

In reparation, above all else, '... the first and most important rule is to do as little as possible compatible with keeping the building in a sound condition.'[3] Colour wash had to be removed from stonework, but it must be done gently and without recutting. Carving was better left unrestored. Repairers were not to be afraid to leave original stones with holes in, for those holes may be a clue to the history of the building. Arcades and walls, where they were leaning or out of true were to be left as long as no pressure was put on them. Individual stones were only to be replaced where really necessary and then to the exact size and with the correct mouldings. This must only be done under the supervision of the architect. No one else could be trusted! In his paper on restoration Fowler implied that, apart from the architect, only the clergy could be trusted to see that old work was not destroyed or tampered with. Even the Clerk of the Works and the builder were suspect. It certainly could not be left to the workmen who were, '... as a matter of course, unlearned and ignorant in matters of art, naturally have but little care for antiquities and cannot appreciate the most interesting work; indeed would frequently destroy it from the feeling, natural to them, that new work is smarter than old.'[4] Such misguided faith in the clergy may be understandable from a member of a clerical family, but his patronising attitude to skilled workmen jars on modern sensibilities. In any case, it can be demonstrated that there are one or two cases in which Fowler himself appears to have believed that, 'new work is smarter and better than old,' especially if the old were Georgian.

In pursuit of reparation rather than restoration, when wet or rotten floors were repaired, all grave slabs were to be retained and relaid on concrete. Medieval stone paving was also to be retained and not replaced with glaring tiles, although these were allowed in new churches where their context made it another matter. If it were really necessary, wet and decayed plaster could be renewed. But, under no circumstances were rubble walls, which were always meant to be plastered, to be left bare and pointed up, leaving the church feeling, 'like a barn.' (If only all later architects had followed this particular piece of advice we would not have quite so many dreary churches!) Fowler's opinion was that this practice was ugly and dirty; '... why, in this much vaunted 19th century people go on committing such a barbarism I cannot tell.'[5]

However, where ashlar was found to be underneath plaster, it was permissible to expose it, but it was only to be flat pointed and not with black mortar, which was a 'vulgar unsightly barbarism.'

A similar attitude was to be taken to woodwork as to masonry. In roofs the repairer was to keep all they could and replace the rest with fresh wood keeping strictly to the sizes and mouldings of the old. There were to be no such modern practices as V joints and diagonal boarding. (Some Bills of Quantity seem to indicate that such things were not allowed in Fowler's new churches either.) Old doors were not to be discarded – they could be spliced and made good. Good examples of this latter advice put into practice by the man himself may be seen at Stillingfleet church, Yorkshire. In any case, he argued that an inner porch or curtain will keep out the cold better than a new door.

Although oak was preferred, the use of pitch pine was not decried, as it could be made to look well with a little dark stain and beeswax, but it must not be varnished as such garishly tasteless practices destroyed the sense of quiet repose given by an old building. Tasteful woodwork of quality is a feature of Fowler's new work but sometimes it has been spoilt by shiny varnish as on the recently mutilated examples at Mumby, Lincolnshire.

For fixtures and fittings the same rules apply, but the newer the artefact the less respect it receives. Large Elizabethan monuments may be shifted a few feet if it allowed the opening up of a blocked medieval door or window. But wall tablets should often be moved, 'to a less conspicuous position.' Old pulpits and organ cases should be kept and reused, even if it was necessary to adapt them. Similarly old altar rails could be retained, even if the gates had to be removed, or they could be moved and used as a low chancel screen.

When windows were releaded or reglazed Fowler recommended the retention and replacement *in situ* of old pieces of glass. Contrary to the advice of some modern architects he also heartily commended the retention or introduction of window ironwork – stanchions and saddle bars. These ferrimenta are a trademark of Fowler's work. He argued that they were a protection to the church and an immense improvement to its look. He also argued that, '... any real artist in glass will tell you how very greatly the effect of their windows is increased by the light and shade given by the ironwork.'[6] Presumably, 'a real artist in glass,' means one of Fowler's own favourites like Burlison and Grylls.

Hodgson Fowler's churchmanship is displayed when he discusses what is to be done with Jacobean or Caroline altar tables, which he felt were not often suitable for their proper use. (Many parish priests may concur.) At best some extra framework could be added to them with a new mensa. A thick stone mensa would both look good and be suitable to an old frame. At worst, '... if the whole is too small for an altar, the old top should be burnt and the frame used as a vestry table.'[7] It might be wondered how such a proposal would fare with our present day Diocesan Advisory Committees.

An excellent and detailed account of how Fowler put these principles into practice, in the churches he restored in the North and East Ridings, is to be found in an unpublished dissertation of 1972, in the Architecture Department of Newcastle University.[8]

Scawton church in North Yorkshire is considered to be an excellent example of his restoration work. Pevsner says, 'A bouquet is due to Hodgson Fowler, who, in 1897, restored the church so tactfully that it now appears as genuine as one can find medieval village churches.'[9] It is a small Norman church which has certainly been restored sympathetically. The low Norman chancel arch and the two arched recesses either side have been treated so that their stonework is exposed in a very effective and attractive way. Yet even this example of restoration in accord with his principles leaves us with what is, in a number of ways, a Fowler church. The flattened interior ceilings hide a high pitched red tiled roof which has, at its west end, a typical Hodgson Fowler bell turret with the normal wooden louvres and a stumpy shingled pointed cap. Fowler's plan of the church, 'as restored in 1897,' shows that

Sympathetic restoration: Scawton, Yorkshire

24

the small Norman window in the west end is his as also is the south porch. The furnishings, although appropriately simple in design, also look like Fowler's, with a wooden screened off vestry at the west, simple stalls, benches, lectern and credence.

A similarly sympathetic and tactful example of Fowler's restoration work, but from a decade later, is to be found at St. Nicholas' Askham in Nottinghamshire. Here the trademarks of his work are to be seen in the red tiled roof, new south porch, screened off western vestry, and alterations to the Decorated east window. The real give-away here, as at so many churches, is his unmistakable arched and gabled heating chimney – an almost certain sign of C. Hodgson Fowler at work.

Good and detailed accounts of Fowler the restorer at work are to be found in his own papers on Stillingfleet and Salton churches.[10]

Restoration or reparation often went hand in hand with new additions. The additions were often the result of new fashions in worship or the increasing demands of Victorian clergy and congregations for comfort. New heating systems gave rise to new heating chambers below ground and Fowler's distinctive chimney, and the inner porches he so often provided were the result of the need to eliminate draughts. The clergy were provided with new vestries furnished with fitted cupboards for robes, a fireplace and sometimes a sink.

The vestry is nearly always associated with a new organ chamber – probably the most common addition made in conjunction with restoration or rebuilding. This was the result of the Victorian fashion for providing organs in even the most humble of village churches and reflected the revolution in church music which included the revival of hymnody and Anglican chant. Hand in hand with this went the newly surpliced male choir, now housed in Hodgson Fowler's new benches and stalls in the chancel, to the north of which was the new organ in its new chamber. So the west gallery became redundant and could be pulled down.

Very often Fowler was called upon to rebuild or add more substantial parts to old churches. This work is more closely related to that in his new churches which is discussed in the next chapter. One example of a very substantial addition can be found at St. John's Kirk Hammerton near York. Here, in 1891, an already existing Saxon church became the south aisle of what was, in effect, a brand new church. A north aisle had been added to the Saxon church c.1200, and the arcade of that date became the south arcade of the new church, and so Fowler grafted the old church on to a new larger Gothic nave and chancel.[11]

At Kirk Hammerton Fowler made no attempt to marry his new work stylistically to that which already existed, but in other places a deliberate attempt was made to do so. An example can be seen in the provision of a new chancel at Kirby Misperton near Pickering in 1875. Here the chancel windows exactly copy those of the nave.

At Hameringham in Lincolnshire Fowler provided a new nave and south aisle of greenstone, which is grafted on to a poor early Victorian brick chancel. Here he reused the existing Early English south arcade.[12] There are numerous other examples of additions designed by Hodgson Fowler. For example, there are new chancels at Northallerton and, well outside his usual sphere of influence, at Coton near Cambridge; a new tower at Flamborough, Yorkshire; a new south aisle at Wanlip, Leicestershire; a north aisle at Sellatyn, Shropshire; a new brick chancel on a completely re-orientated church at South Ferriby, Lincolnshire. This is but a tiny sample from a large volume of work.

Sometimes it is difficult to know where additions end and complete rebuilds begin. The latter result in what are, in effect, complete new churches. At South Kyme in Lincolnshire an attractive new church was created by Fowler when he rebuilt a church made from a small fragment of an Augustinian priory church. What remains of the latter is the west wall of the south aisle, three bays of the south wall of the same aisle, which contains two very fine Decorated windows, and a south porch. Everything else is Fowler's work, i.e. a new north wall, new chancel with Perpendicular east window, and a further bay to the south wall, which contains an identical copy of the existing medieval windows. He also, of course, provided the attractive and slightly unusual furnishings.[13]

It may be asked how successful Hodgson Fowler was in being truthful to his own principles, and, in general, it has to be asserted that he was. Commentators since his time seem to agree that his work in church restoration was largely successful. Dr. Cox's Little Guide for Lincolnshire, published in 1916, says:

> If we are competent to form an opinion, we feel confident in saying that the work of the late Mr. Hodgson Fowler was always good and conservative.[14]

More recently in the introduction to the County Durham volume in the Buildings of England series we read:

Between 1864 and 1895 C. Hodgson Fowler did a vast number of restorations, handling them sensitively but not slavishly.[15]

The last phrase, 'sensitively but not slavishly,' sums things up rather well. Fowler himself admitted his shortcomings:

> I must say that I am quite aware that you may find works of mine where I have done things I now condemn.[16]

However, in passing judgement on him and his work, the state in which many Victorian architects found the churches they were called upon to restore must be borne in mind. Fowler described an hypothetical example:

> You will most likely find the church with all its internal stonework covered with colour wash, the walls damp and in many places out of the perpendicular and cut for galleries or pews, the floors decayed where boarded and wet where paved, while, outside, the strings and mouldings will be broken and knocked off, the earth heaped up round the walls, and the tracery perhaps gone.[17]

Faced with similar situations, Hodgson Fowler usually successfully negotiated a course which avoided over-restoration, thereby destroying ancient and valuable work, but which still provided a suitable building for the celebration of the Church's liturgy as its needs were felt in the late 19th century.

It has already been shown that Fowler decried the work of those who had destroyed good old work in the name of 'restoring' what they often wrongly imagined had existed originally, but he was also critical of those who had in turn over-reacted to this style of restoration. Whilst finding many of the organisation's aims admirable, he was critical of the leadership of the newly formed Society for the Protection of Ancient Buildings. (In his paper on restoration he inadvertently called it, 'The Society for the Preservation of Ancient Monuments.') He accuses them of forgetting the purpose of church buildings, forgetting that churches were built for divine worship, and treating them simply as monuments. In his paper on the church at Salton, Yorkshire, Fowler had written:

> ... 'restoration,' a work which however much some may dislike and condemn is yet in some degree or other absolutely

necessary if the buildings are to be retained in a state suitable
for the holy uses for which they were originally built.[18]

It is worth quoting the final paragraph of Fowler's paper on restoration at
length, for it points to his motivation not only in restoring or adding to old
churches, but also in designing new ones:

> I ... look on them firstly as God's houses, to be kept in order
> for His honour; and that can, I believe, be done quite
> consistently with preserving all their historical and
> architectural interest ... Good as the Society's (S.P.A.B.'s)
> object may be, it is ruined by this, that its members seem to
> have no care for churches as such, and therefore I, as a
> churchman, cannot belong to it; but though I cannot belong
> to this Society, I deny most strongly that I am in any way
> more destructive than its members; on the contrary, I feel
> that restoration such as I have advocated is truer preservation
> than the Society's 'let alone' theory, which must end in
> destruction.[19]

In modern terms, C. Hodgson Fowler was a conservationist rather than a
preservationist, and his restored churches demonstrate it admirably.

CHAPTER FOUR
The New Churches

In this context, 'new' churches includes the following:

a) all churches, chapels and mission churches designed by Hodgson Fowler for new sites,

b) all churches designed to replace old ones which were to be demolished, as at Revesby and Flixborough in Lincolnshire,

c) complete new churches added to existing towers, as at Faldingworth in Lincolnshire, and Hampsthwaite in Yorkshire,

d) churches completely rebuilt perhaps retaining some masonry, but no detail from the old church, as at Toft next Newton, Lincolnshire.

All of these are, in effect, completely new churches designed by C. Hodgson Fowler.

Not included in this consideration are churches rebuilt so as to include significant features, other than the tower, from the old church, as at the Lincolnshire churches of Greetham, Hameringham and South Kyme, although these are in many ways Fowler churches. The church at Sturton-le-Steeple in Nottinghamshire has not been included as, although, with the exception of the tower, it was completely rebuilt by Fowler after a disastrous fire, the form and design of the new church was largely determined by the old work it replaced. On the other hand, St. Saviour's, Ravensthorpe, in the West Riding, has been included. Although it consists of a grand east end by Fowler grafted on to a nave and south aisle by John Cory of Carlisle, Fowler's work was part of a design for an impressive complete new church which was sadly never completed.

Using these criteria, more than sixty new churches or chapels designed by Hodgson Fowler may be identified. (see Appendix 1.) As with the rest of his work, the vast majority of these are to be found in Co. Durham, Yorkshire, Lincolnshire and Nottinghamshire. There are 'strays' at St. Ambrose Bournemouth, St. Augustine's Belvedere (Kent), St. Paul's College Chapel Cheltenham, Christ Church Hepple (Northumberland), and St. Columb's Notting Hill (now St. Sava's Serbian Church.)

Early Churches and Early English

Those who have become familiar with Fowler's work through his work in Yorkshire or Lincolnshire, or those who take his published papers as a guide, may be surprised by the breadth of style displayed in his work elsewhere.

The group of churches designed by Hodgson Fowler in his twenties for parishes in Co. Durham all have the feel of the work of men of an earlier generation, and are recognisably the work of someone under the influence of Gilbert Scott. The churches at Leadgate, Harton, East Rainton, Haswell and Tow Law all display Early English details with lancets, sometimes with attached shafts and sometimes grouped, wheel windows and plate tracery.

Probably the most successful of these early churches is at Tow Law, but the biggest is at Leadgate. Begun in 1865 this is a plain stone church of nave, aisles (the north added in 1879), and chancel with organ chamber and vestry to the north. It has a nave of five bays with round pillars, square abaci, and unmoulded and unchamfered arches. The double chamfered chancel arch ends, typically for Fowler, in Early English carved corbels. The clerestory has round windows of pierced plate tracery with arched openings inside, and the aisles are lit by low lancets. The east window feels unbalanced with three stepped lights, having strange trefoil openings above the side lights. At the west end there are two lancets under a wheel window of pierced plate tracery.

This is all in a style with which one feels Fowler himself would not have been happy fifteen years later. Also in the 1860s he built a church of rock-faced masonry at St. Peter's Harton (South Shields), and he did it again a decade later at Holy Trinity Murton and at St. Mary's Middleton-in-Teesdale. This is rather strange because, only a short while later, he spoke of, '... what is, I believe, called rock-work, the sort of rough walling so dear to railway engineers, but altogether out of character in an old church.'[1] – And, by implication, in any decent church?

The Early English is a style Fowler later abandoned, although it is interesting that he retained it in new work in Co. Durham well after he had abandoned it elsewhere. Both St. Paul's Hartlepool of 1885 and St. Ignatius Hendon (Sunderland) of 1889 are large churches, in plan and atmosphere like his large churches further south, but both still have Early English detail.

The church at Hartlepool is described by Pevsner as, '... one of (Fowler's) most expensive and successful efforts in the county.'[2] It is a very lofty red brick church with the emphasis all on the vertical. There is a tall slim north west tower and a lofty nave with low aisles. There are double

30

lancets in the aisles and clerestory, five stepped-up lancets at the east end, and three lancets with a wheel window above them at the west end. The north transept has three stepped-down lancets again with a wheel above. There is an attractive Early English sedilia with shafts of Purbeck marble. Marble and alabaster feature elsewhere in the church, as in the pulpit and font. The overall effect is rather grand but, because of the bare brick and unpainted woodwork, perhaps a little too dark for modern taste.

1880s Early English: St Paul's Hartlepool

St. Ignatius Hendon is even later in date than St. Paul's Hartlepool, and yet still has Early English detail. It is again a lofty church with a strong vertical emphasis, but this time in stone and with a south west tower surmounted by a broach spire. Local lore has it that it was one of Fowler's own favourites. It is certainly a splendid building, impressively simple, and, in feel, rather akin to a sizeable church by J.L. Pearson. It must have been even more impressive when Fowler's original scheme of painting and stencilling still existed. The modern colour scheme is not completely successful and the modern floor tiles are definitely inappropriate.

St Ignatius Hendon, Sunderland

As at Hartlepool, the arcades have quatrefoil pillars, and again the clerestory has double lancets. The aisles have low single lancets to the north and double to the south. There are three stepped lancets above a large stone reredos at the east end, and three level lancets at the west end. The clerestory of the chancel has blank arcading either side of a single lancet, giving an effect almost like a triforium.

Further south, where the churches were built later, it is difficult to find a Fowler church with any early English detail after 1880. As previously noted, the early 1880s mark a turning point in Fowler's personal and professional life as well as a watershed stylistically.

During the first half of the 1870s much of his attention must have been given to the restoration work at Durham Cathedral, but the new work carried out in the North East towards the end of that decade still bears the marks of his early work with Early English detail. In this respect, Holy Trinity Murton looks as though it could have been designed in the 1860s, although its unsatisfactory composition is a result of its never having been completed as designed, with a north aisle and further bay to the uncomfortably short chancel. A quarter of a century later Fowler was to achieve something far more satisfying on a similar hillside site at Thurlstone in Yorkshire.

The brick church at Bearpark near Durham is also from this period. It looks like a church designed by an architect constrained to provide a given number of sittings on a very tight budget. The exterior is extremely plain and the nave is lit by double brick lancets. In the chancel a little more expense is allowed, the south wall having a row of lancets with stone detail including interior shafts. The east wall has a similar treatment – three stepped lancets with a lower blank arch either side. The west end has an unusual arrangement whereby the stumpy brick tower and spirelet rise from the nave roof, supported internally on three crude brick arches. There is a similar but more successful arrangement in stone at Upper Poppleton near York but designed a decade later. Here a similar short tower and cap are supported internally on three graceful stepped arches – a good effect.

Designed just after Bearpark, at the very end of the 1870s, is the church at South Hylton, Sunderland. It also has Early English detail with three conventional stepped lancets at the east end. But here there are hints of what is to come in both the two bay arcade into the north chapel (with quatrefoil pillar), and in the windows which have a variation on Y tracery.

The Nottinghamshire Factor

If given dates are to be believed, the mould had been broken as early as 1879, when Hodgson Fowler built the new church at Middleton-in-Teesdale. It seems that a stylistic shift, from the Early English to the adoption of late Decorated and Perpendicular, comes after Fowler prepared his paper on, 'Some Characteristics of Nottinghamshire Churches,' which was delivered in St. Swithin's church at East Retford. It was published in the Associated Architectural Societies Report and Papers Vol.XV in 1880. Despite his protestations that he had not had time to prepare properly for the paper, it is clear that he had done a lot of work, and in particular he had made an extensive architectural tour of his native county. He noted that he had visited a good many churches new to him as well as renewing his acquaintance with others.[3]

Fowler noted that Nottinghamshire churches shared much stylistically with those of the surrounding counties, but there were certain features which were characteristic of that county's churches. It must be more than coincidence that, after undertaking the research for this paper, these same features became part of his own stylistic portfolio in his new chuches.

Those from south of the Tees, who are not familiar with Fowler's pre-1880 work in Co. Durham, might think that his work is universally late-Decorated or Perpendicular in style, and in, 'Nottinghamshire Churches,' he wrote:

> ... one of the most characteristic features of Nottinghamshire churches is the quantity of good late or 'Flowing Decorated' work, and especially in the latest period of the style when the influence of the coming Perpendicular was making itself felt.[4]

He went on to speak of the well known examples of rich work in this style at Newark, Hawton and elsewhere, and then he continued:

> ... I would ... now speak of what I believe is not so generally known, the great variety and beauty of the late Decorated work of a simple kind, than which I can conceive nothing more beautiful and appropriate for our village churches containing, as it does, good construction, beauty of design,

fitness for its position, and what I know must be an object with many; great moderation in cost.[5]

This could be taken as Hodgson Fowler's manifesto for much of his work in new churches for the next thirty years. Much of it has this 'Nottinghamshire Factor.'

Even in his early immature work Fowler's style was unmistakably English, and in this paper he could not resist a side-swipe at some architects of the preceding generation. He praised this late Decorated work as thoroughly English, 'and much better-suited to our country scenery than the incongruous mixture of so-called Early French and other continental styles that unfortunately here and there disfigure the country.'[6]

Fowler describes two kinds of windows of this simple late Decorated Nottinghamshire style, one square headed and the other pointed. The former were invariably used in side walls, and the latter also in end walls. He notes that square headed windows of this date and style are far more abundant in Nottinghamshire than in any other district with which he was acquainted. This has been noted by others and such windows have sometimes been described as being of a Nottinghamshire type even when they occur elsewhere. Fowler illustrated his paper with cleanly drawn examples. These show features of tracery seen after the late 1870s in his own new work. For example, tracery of a pattern illustrated from Keyworth is found in the clerestory of St. Oswald's Hebburn, Co. Durham, whilst in the same church, the south chancel windows are very similar to the pattern illustrated from West Bridgford.

The paper is also illustrated with examples of simple late Decorated windows of an arched type. Again his own later work bears resemblance to the examples given. The chancel and south chapel of Fowler's church at St. Peter's Norton, Yorkshire, have windows strikingly similar to the medieval example shown from Car Colston in Nottinghamshire.

Fowler's churches are full of examples of simple pointed late Decorated windows with distinctive and recognisable tracery patterns of an individual style probably not found in any medieval building. An extremely simple example, which occurs frequently, is a biggish three light window, with the centre light reaching to the apex and simple cusping to each light and in the spandrels. Good examples are to be found in the clerestories of All Saints Lincoln and St. Alban's Ordsall, Nottinghamshire, and in the south wall of the chancel at Easington in the North Riding. A five light version is to be found in the east window of St. Barnabas' Crosland Moor, Huddersfield. A variation on this pattern, with dagger motifs above the side

35

lights, is to be found in the aisle windows at Crosland Moor and at Thurlstone, as well as in the east window at St. John's Bracebridge Heath, Lincoln.

Window design was not always simple. There are beautiful examples of much more complex Decorated tracery in the east windows at All Saints Lincoln, Revesby (Lincs.), Norton (Yorks.), and a startling early example at Middleton-in-Teesdale. Yet simplicity was more often the case. Frequently found in Fowler's work are two or three light windows with simple reticulated tracery as at Faldingworth and Revesby in Lincolnshire and St. Helen's Grove in Nottinghamshire.

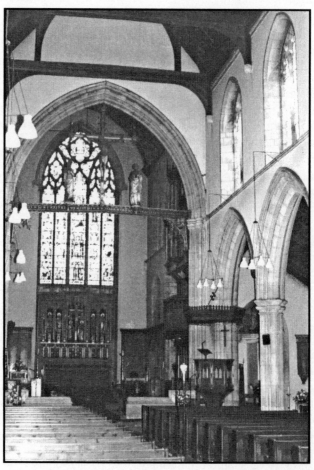

Unostentatious dignity at All Saints, Lincoln

36

St. Mary's, Middleton-in-Teesdale (Co. Durham), of 1879, is particularly significant in the stylistic development of Hodgson Fowler's new church work. It is in some ways transitional between the old and the new, the immature and the mature. Lofty, and of a familiar plan – nave, aisles, south porch, and chancel with organ chamber and vestry to the north – it has four bay arcades with octagonal piers and double chamfered arches, and, above these, a clerestory of late Decorated Nottinghamshire square-headed type. But the external walls are of rock-faced masonry, and the windows of the aisles and chancel are of late 13th century pattern with Y tracery (like their contemporaries at South Hylton.) Old photographs show that this matches the style of the chancel windows in the old church. The west window has simple intersecting tracery of a similar stylistic date. The most startling feature is the east window. A strikingly original affair for its date, it is divided unequally by two sturdy mullions which reach the whole length of the window, and it has a very attractive tracery pattern of quatrefoils and mouchettes. With its Kempe glass this window is a composition which one might expect to find twenty years later. Overall the building has an experimental feel about it, and, unusually for Fowler, lacks unity.

This cannot be said of the church at Grove, Nottinghamshire, which was built only two years later. Although not large, it also is of significance in the stylistic development of Hodgson Fowler's work. It is a limestone church with a tall narrow nave and chancel with the usual organ chamber and vestry to the north. There is a south porch and a very pleasing tower with recessed spire. Its significance lies in that it is Fowler's first thorough-going essay in the late Decorated. It is also one of the first of his new churches in which the impression is given that Fowler was not being constrained by a tight budget. Everything is of restrained good taste and high quality. There is glass by Burlison and Grylls, and much of Fowler's own woodwork. The latter includes a barrel vaulted ceiling to the chancel, more richly carved over the sanctuary than elsewhere. The excellent detail includes a traceried door to the sacristy which is set in a depressed ogee arch. It is appropriate that this significant church is in Nottinghamshire, a survey of which county's churches seems to have encouraged Hodgson Fowler to stylistic development in his own work.

A very similar but larger church is to be found at St. Laurence, Revesby, in Lincolnshire where the Wolds meet the Fen. It was designed eight years later than Grove, but has many similar features and, this time, a north aisle. Approached from the east along the road from Spilsby, the eye is first caught by the tower and spire (of a type more to be expected in Northamptonshire), and then by the excellent composition and proportions

1880s Decorated: Revesby, Lincs.

of this building. The Shell Guide to Lincolnshire, and a later book based upon it, describe this church as, 'expensively dull,' and yet go on to praise as, 'more exciting,' the one jarring note in the whole building – a crude and sentimental Art Nouveau reredos.[7] In the past the restrained good taste of the late Victorian period has sometimes been mistaken for dullness by those who are impressed by the polychromatic excesses of the earlier Victorians.

After 1880 the Perpendicular style also became important in Hodgson Fowler's work – as important as the late Decorated. In his latest work, the styles are often mixed. For example, at St. Saviour's Ravensthorpe, Yorkshire, the large north window of the north transept has simple Perpendicular bar tracery in its lower panels with tracery of an earlier style in the arch.

In his paper on Church Restoration, Fowler wrote these words about the Perpendicular style:

> ... whatever opinion may be held as to the suitability of Perpendicular for stone work – and I hold that it is, with its comparatively thin walls, ample windows, and general features, most fitted for our use – there can be no doubt whatever that as applied to woodwork it is by far the best of the Gothic styles. The deep hollow round mouldings of the earlier styles are perfectly legitimate in stone, but in wood they are not suited to the material.... But the thin tracery and mouldings of Perpendicular work are exactly suited to the material, and always have a most excellent effect.[8]

Amongst the bigger churches designed by Hodgson Fowler in a Perpendicular style, or with Perpendicular detail, are St. Alban's Ordsall (Notts.), the Chapel of St. Paul's College, Cheltenham, St. Aidan's Cleethorpes (Lincs.), and St. Andrew's Bishopthorpe near York. The latter is the parish church of the Archbishops of York, and they paid for its rebuilding. Two particularly attractive, and stylistically closely related, examples are at St. Faith's Lincoln, and St. Aidan's Grangetown (Sunderland.) Both are brick churches with stone dressings.

St. Faith's was designed in the 1880s. It is a little-known gem, occupying a cramped urban site, but giving the impression of a bigger church than it is, being almost as wide as it is long. There is a nave of three bays with octagonal pillars and castellated capitals, and a chancel of two bays with arcades having clustered pillars. The aisles run the full length of the building and have high pitched roofs almost as high as that of the nave. The aisles have big four light Perpendicular windows which are set in brick arches – an idiosyncratic feature seen also in the brick churches at New Holland and Woodhall Spa (also in Lincs.) There is no clerestory, but the division between nave and chancel is marked by dormer windows which, on either side, light the rood. One of the delights of St. Faith's is that nearly all the woodwork is contemporary and therefore by Fowler. There is a large reredos, recently garishly painted with too much dark blue, and sadly lacking its original tryptich doors. There are screens to the chancel and chapels, but the most remarkable feature for its date is that the rood and its figures are original and therefore by Fowler. The overall effect is to provide a church fit for the most advanced Anglican Catholic worship, as its needs were understood in the 1880s.

The church at Grangetown is very similar in plan and detail, but it lacks a rood screen and is of 25 years later. Its foundation stone was laid in September 1910, only three months before Hodgson Fowler's death, and it was therefore finished much later, to Fowler's design, but under the supervision of his successor, W.H.Wood.

Many of Fowler's smaller churches, especially the brick ones, have Perpendicular detail, but sometimes used in a very free manner. Two charming examples are to be found in Yorkshire at St. Chad's Great Habton of 1884 and St. Lawrence's Carlton Minniott of 1896. Great Habton is a delightful little church of brick with stone dressings, having nave and chancel under one high pitched roof with a bellcote at the west end. There are simple two and three light straight headed Perpendicular windows to north and south with a good pointed Perpendicular window to the west, but, unusually, no east window of any kind. Inside there is a simple Perpendicular screen between nave and chancel. It has roses and other foliage carved in the spandrels. The clergy stalls are simple but unmistakably by Hodgson Fowler, and there is an octagonal font with shields on four faces. The usual boarded ceiling is provided for the chancel. It is a homely but worthy setting for the worship of a small village community. In one of Fowler's sketchbooks, dated 1881, there is a sketch for an unnamed small church which is undoubtedly Great Habton.[9]

Carlton Minniott has another charming church of twelve years later. It is slightly larger than Great Habton, but again has nave and chancel under one roof, this time with a large wooden bellcote and stumpy spirelet over the divide. Again the side walls have square headed windows of two and three lights, but this time without cusping or even hoodmoulds – a very pleasing effect. The west window is Perpendicular, again without cusping, but the east window is a more disappointing effort of three stepped lights. Internally, once again there is a chancel screen with Perpendicular tracery. Most pleasing of all is the painted and stencilled chancel ceiling – a rare survivor of Fowler's decorative work and not in good condition. Hopefully some way may be found to conserve it.

A rare survival: painted and stencilled chancel ceiling at Carlton Minniott

Although his early churches had Early English detail, the majority of Fowler's new churches and chapels are in his favoured late Decorated or Perpendicular styles. The present writer knows of no complete new church which he designed in Norman style, although at Copmanthorpe, Yorkshire, he designed additions in that style to match existing work.

Fowler was in many ways a man of his time, and, like many Victorian church architects, what he most despised was the Georgian style of the 18th and early 19th centuries. In his paper on Glentworth church (Lincs.), published in 1877, he described how the old nave, aisle and porch had been destroyed in 1782 on the instructions of the Archdeacon, to be rebuilt, 'in its present hideous form.'[10] Elsewhere he expressed similar sentiments about Georgian church furnishings. There are a number of examples where Georgian churches were demolished to make way for new Gothic buildings designed by Fowler. Two examples in Lincolnshire are at All Saints Flixborough and Ss. Peter and Paul Toft-next-Newton (now a private residence.) In both cases, however, Fowler made plans of the existing churches before they were demolished and rebuilt.

The Basilicas

The most surprising new churches designed by Hodgson Fowler are the Romanesque basilicas. They are the 'jokers in the pack,' and are stylistically so different from the rest of his work that it is difficult to believe that they are, indeed, by him. But perhaps we should not be too surprised, for the key lies in churchmanship – they are all undoubtedly places of Catholic worship. All four are of brick. All four are large. There is a monumental aspect to them all.

The earliest in date (1888-90), and probably the best, is St. Columba's Southwick (Sunderland.) it has a large wide nave with arcades of eight bays to the south and seven to the north, the eighth being occupied by the organ loft. There is an apse to the east, and, at the west end, an apsidal baptistery which is encompassed by a low porch/narthex running the width of the building There is a clerestory of double lights, and the narrow aisles are lit by smaller single lights. A low marble wall marks the steps up to the choir, and there are marble pavements in the sanctuary.

The second of Fowler's basilican churches is in London. What used to be St. Columb's Notting Hill dates from 1901. It is built of white brick laid in English bond, and is crammed into a very tight site which allows only a view of the west end with its round window high up. The external effect is frankly ugly, as the west end has been ruined in recent years by the demolition of the baptistery. Internally the effect is very different and quite moving. As at Southwick, the impression is of space, width and height. The very narrow aisles have access only through two Romanesque arches either side of the nave. Again there is a low marble wall at the steps to the choir, and a splendid baldachino over the high altar. This church is now known as St. Sava's, and is used by the Serbian community. It makes quite a good Orthodox church, but the overall effect is spoiled somewhat by the way in which the baldichino now peeps over the new iconostasis.

Romanesque basilica: St Columba's Southwick, Sunderland

The church of Ss. Hilda and Helen, Dawdon, at Seaham in Co. Durham is another striking basilica. Like the church at Grangetown in Sunderland, the foundation stone was laid only three months before Hodgson Fowler's death, and it was therefore completed by W.H. Wood who designed a baldachino which was never erected.[11] Yet again it is a big church but this time with very simple brick arcades and also transverse brick arches over the narrow aisles, which produce a tunnel-like effect. There is an apse at the east end and another to the north chapel. With a large round window over a long low narthex at the west end, the effect externally is similar to Southwick. The church and its furnishing are thoroughly Edwardian in a most attractive way.

There is yet another church which almost certainly belongs to this group. That is at St. Augustine's Belvedere in Kent. Pevsner says that this church was built by Temple Moor to the designs of Hodgson Fowler, a start being made in 1911. However the parish's own Diamond Jubilee pamphlet gave the architect as T.C. Dewey. The church appears to have many features in common with those described above, and especially Dawdon. The fact that a note about it appears in the penultimate of Fowler's notebooks[12], would also lead to the conclusion that it belongs to his family of basilicas.

Three Significant Churches

No account of Hodgson Fowler's new churches would be complete without particular note of three outstanding buildings, at Norton and Marsden in Yorkshire, and at Lincoln.

Although there are weaknesses internally, externally St. Peter's Norton in the East Riding is probably the most successful and impressive of Fowler's new churches. This is partly because its surroundings, especially to the south, are comparatively open, and therefore, although it is a large church, it may be appreciated as a whole. There is an impressive west tower, nave, aisles, south porch, and chancel with south chapel and, to the north, a gabled organ chamber and vestry – a common Hodgson Fowler plan. The church is of stone, and the windows are filled with excellent reticulated or flowing tracery. Inside there are arcades of five bays with octagonal pillars and double chamfered arches. To the west, as is so often the case in Fowler's bigger churches, the arcades do not go up to the west wall, but, instead, there is a short piece of walling at their west end, which is itself then pierced by another smaller arch. There are two arches to the south chapel, and an organ loft to the north. The effect internally is not as effective because it is all rather bare. The nave walls are plastered and whitened, but the chancel is of stark grey ashlar, and lacks the richly carved reredos and other pious furnishings with which a congregation of more Catholic leaning might have furnished it. However, the Kempe glass helps to soften the effect.

Norton church was begun in 1896, but not completed until after Fowler's death. Nevertheless, a print showing a completed church hangs in the nave and proudly proclaims C. Hodgson Fowler F.S.A. as its architect.

Of St. Bartholomew's church, Marsden, he had reason to be even more proud. The present writer considers it one of his two masterpieces. It is of a similar date to Norton (1895) and of a similar plan, but Perpendicular

Powerful architecture at St Bartholomew's, Marsden

in style and more grand. The nave, with arcades of six bays and clustered pillars, is of cathedral-like proportions, and the effect of grandeur is enhanced by the good quality ashlar stonework. There is much rich woodwork in reredos, screen and rood, all added later, but the excellent clergy stalls and choir seating are by Fowler, and of a pattern so reminiscent of his work. The Perpendicular stone pulpit and font are also by him. Between the south aisle and south chapel are two cusped arches under a bigger arch with flat tracery and an image niche in the tympanum. A similar arrangement can be found at the entrance to the north chapel at Ravensthorpe, and between the north aisle and organ chamber at Revesby. The impression is of architecture which, in accord with Fowler's own spirituality, puts human beings in their rightful place before God – on their knees!

In criticising the design of many pews and congregational benches, Fowler quoted Psalm 95:

> ... my Prayer Book has much about kneeling, but not a word of sitting, ... we ought, above all, and before all, to remember that we are invited, and it is our duty to, 'worship and fall down, and kneel before the Lord our Maker'.[13]

Marsden church impresses that 'duty' upon the worshipper.

Of a decade later is the church at All Saints, Lincoln. Unlike Norton and Marsden, it has no tower, and is of brick with stone dressings externally, with stone dressings and plastered walls internally. If the effect at Marsden is to force us to our knees by its grandeur, at All Saints, with its late 14th century detail, we are brought to our knees by the simple beauty of holiness. There is a long lofty nave with arcades of five bays with quatrefoil pillars. A high clerestory has windows of a common pattern already noted, and the low aisles have simple single cusped lights. The whole composition leads the eye inexorably eastwards to the chancel and to the focus of the high altar. There, beneath a beautifully proportioned tall east window of reticulated tracery, is Fowler's carved reredos with its saints, later coloured and gilded so appropriately by Ninian Comper.

The effect is heightened by the fact that later generations have not erected a chancel screen, but instead, entirely appropriately, a rood beam with its rood and attendant figures of our Lady and St. John, designed by Ninian Comper, was inserted high up in the chancel arch. The chancel has clergy stalls and choir benches in Fowler's familiar and tasteful style, and to the south there is an organ loft with a charming small chapel beneath it. To the north of the chancel is a transept with a north chapel to the east of it, entered through a double arched opening. The literal crowning glory of the chancel is its elaborately painted and stencilled ceiling, which should be preserved at all costs.

The whole emphasis of this building is on the vertical, no more so than in the way in which Fowler conceived the west wall. Here there are three very tall and graceful windows of equal height, divided externally by buttresses, and having in their heads a simple but elegant pattern of reticulated tracery. Above these windows is another small square one with a hoodmould and containing a quatrefoil.

The vertical loftiness of this church is anchored to the ground by the low aisles and the vestries to the east. Internally there are ever changing vistas displaying the imagination and technical brilliance of an architect at the height of his powers and the peak of his career. All Saints, Lincoln, is an unsung and unknown masterpiece.

Typical Hodgson Fowler woodwork at All Saints, Lincoln

CHAPTER FIVE
Some Characteristics of Hodgson Fowler's Churches

As will be understood from the above account of his new work, there is no such thing as a, 'typical Hodgson Fowler church.' Although most of his mature work is late Decorated and Perpendicular in feel and detail, there is both the work of his twenties and thirties in Early English style, and the later impressive Romanesque basilicas, in which the Gothic was completely abandoned. Yet, as a clergyman from the diocese of Durham remarked, 'There is something characteristic about an Hodgson Fowler church once you know he has been involved.' The clues to that characteristic nature may lie in oft-repeated details or in factors less easily defined and more subjectively aesthetic.

Although Fowler used both stone and brick in construction, he used them in a variety of ways. There are churches with ashlared interiors, as at Bishopthorpe and Marsden, plastered interiors too numerous to mention, and bare brick interiors, as at Hartlepool and Woodhall Spa. Most of the brick churches have stone detail, although in a few cases there is brick tracery, as at New Holland and Woodhall Spa. The brick churches seem nearly always to be built in English Bond or, in cheaper churches, English Garden Wall Bond. At Sykehouse the interior walls are in Flemish Bond, although the outer are in English Bond.

There are a number of characteristic trademarks in style and detail. Many of them are of course shared with other architects, but a number of them together on a building are clues to Fowler's authorship. For example, the coping stones on gables will often end at the eaves with a little cusped triangular stone, like a mini-gable. Often the detail of a vestry, to the north of the chancel, will have a decidedly more domestic feel than the rest of the building, with square headed, even untraceried, windows and a doorway with a shouldered arch. Good examples of this characteristic are found at Tudhoe Grange, Co. Durham, and Crosland Moor, Huddersfield. Often associated with the vestry will be a sure sign of Hodgson Fowler at work – his unique chimney to a vestry fireplace or heating system. This has, at the top, an arch under a gable.

In roof coverings Fowler was more sensitive than some architects to locality. Cumbrian slates are often used in the north and red tiles further south, but this split is not universal. At High Hoyland, in the Yorkshire hills, he used the large stone slates of the Pennines.

If there is a 'typical' Hodgson Fowler ground plan, it consists basically of a nave and chancel with, to the north, an organ chamber, and, to the east of that, a vestry. A chancel screen will probably have been part of the plan only in a small church, as at Great Habton or St. John's Bracebridge Heath, where sadly it has been removed. To this basic plan may be added a porch (usually to the south). There may be an aisle or aisles, and, in larger churches, a south chapel. If there is a tower, it is invariably to the west or at one of the west corners. This was true even of the unfinished churches, where towers were planned but never built, as at Thurlstone and Ravensthorpe.

Although most of Hodgson Fowler's new churches did not run to towers, the most common feature of his work is a distinctive bell turret, either at the west end of the nave roof, or over the division between nave and chancel. These vary somewhat in design, but all belong to the same family. Usually there are wooden louvres to the sides, and sometimes there is wooden Perpendicular tracery to the bell openings. Most are square, but some are octagonal, and they are surmounted by pointed caps, which are slate-hung or shingled, and which vary in length from a stumpy pyramid, as at Carlton Minniott, to an elegant fleche, as at All Saints Lincoln. Another pleasing example is the octagonal spirelet at Romanby near Northallerton.

Some of the most distinctive features of Fowler's churches are found in their woodwork and its decoration. In early churches he had attempted what he later regarded as a futile exercise – to design furniture in Early English style, as in the pulpit at South Hylton. His most characteristic furniture has late Decorated or Perpendicular details, and certain motifs occur repeatedly, notably certain dagger or mouchette motifs. One of the most recognisable patterns occurs frequently in choir stalls and clergy stalls. It consists of a quatrefoil roundel with interlocking elongated daggers or mouchettes on either side. Good examples are in the choir benches at Hampsthwaite (Yorks.), and St. Faith's, Lincoln. As well as these motifs, it is quite common to find that the boys' (front) desks are of an open design finished with a depressed ogee, as at Grove and Bearpark. Clergy stalls are often finished in even richer detail.

Lecterns and pulpits are similarly treated. There are especially good wooden pulpits at Thurlstone and All Saints, Lincoln, and a particularly good example in stone at Marsden. Fonts are also usually fitting to the building, from the tub font at Harton, South Shields, to the panelled Perpendicular example at Marsden. The font at St. Paul's Hartlepool is splendidly appropriate to its setting – an alabaster and marble affair, in which the octagonal basin sits atop a central shaft which is surrounded by detached shafts.

Pulpit of All Saints, Lincoln

As was the case at Marsden, sometimes Fowler's new churches were provided with chairs for congregational seating, and these have been replaced at a later date by heavier pews. Fowler's own pews or congregational benches were not usually of a heavy design, normally having an open back-rest below a horizontal bar. As has been noted, what mattered to Fowler was that pews were designed so that people could (and should) kneel. He never seems to have placed his congregational seats on raised wooden platforms, as is the annoying habit in so many Victorian churches. They were placed on the floor which, under seats, was boarded or, in later or more expensive churches, made of wooden blocks.

Doors are often treated distinctively by Hodgson Fowler. A common form is an oak door on which simply moulded wooden beading, with prominent nailheads, runs lengthways over the iron hinges. Examples are many, but two may be found at Grove, one in the south door and another in the door to the organ chamber. Often doors are designed to

Door and doorway at Grove

complement the doorway in which they stand. The results can be beautiful. An excellent example is the sacristy door at Bishopthorpe near York, where a door with flat Perpendicular tracery stands in a 15th century style doorway which has carved fleurons all the way round its hollow jambs and arch and a hoodmould with carved head labelstops. Similar very attractive doorways can be found in the south porch of the same church, at Marsden, Crosland Moor and Ravensthorpe. Another fine example of this union of door and doorway is to be found in the door to the sacristy at Grove. Often in Fowler's churches the main entrance is provided with an inner porch. These can be quite substantial affairs. On the other hand, the congregation may be protected from draughts simply by a curtain hanging from an ogee arched pelmet.

Door and doorway at Bishopthorpe

Roofs are also a distinctive feature of his new churches. Chancel ceilings are often barrel vaulted (never boarded diagonally), whilst nave roofs are left open. There are, of course exceptions to this general rule, as in the

52

chancel at Upper Poppleton and the naves of High Hoyland and St. Paul's Hartlepool. Apart from over aisles, the roofs of Hodgson Fowler's new churches are invariably high pitched, even in Perpendicular churches where something flatter might sometimes have been expected. If the chancel ceiling was not originally painted and stencilled, it will often be more rich in its mouldings and carved bosses over the sanctuary, as at Hampsthwaite and Grove. The timbering of open nave roofs is often distinctive in design. The typical nave roof of a larger Fowler church has a hefty tie beam supported on braced wall posts resting on corbels. Above the tie beam are queen posts with an arched brace up to a collar. This common form, or a slight variation on it, may be found at Marsden, Norton, All Saints Lincoln, Bishopthorpe, Hebburn and West Harton (South Shields). Other arrangements are found. Sometimes the tie beam is replaced by hammer beams, and sometimes there is a king post, but always the construction is obvious and substantial.

If the stained glass is contemporary or in keeping, it will be by a firm favoured by Fowler. Perhaps it will be by Kempe as at Norton, or, even more likely, by Burlison and Grylls. The work of the latter firm complements Fowler's work so well. See the Anunciation in the south window at Grove, and a very similar treatment of the same subject in the south chapel at Bishopthorpe. Fowler's memorial window in St. Oswald's church, Durham, although attributed by some to Kempe and Co., is actually signed, 'B.& G.,' and dated 1911.

It is now difficult to appreciate how some of Fowler's churches would originally have appeared, for they had painted and stencilled schemes of decoration to walls and ceilings which have since disappeared. What has sadly been lost and never restored can be seen in old photographs, of which there are examples at All Saints West Harton (South Shields), and at St. Ignatius Hendon (Sunderland). Fowler's original drawings give a hint of what is lost in the chancel at St. Faiths, Lincoln[1], a church which suffered badly from an act of vandalism and arson in the 1970s. Chancel roof decoration survives at Carlton Minniott, All Saints Lincoln, and, surprisingly, at Flixborough (Lincs.) – a church which has otherwise suffered the all too common indignity of redecoration with pale blue paint. Sadly, too many of Fowler's churches have been cheapened and disfigured by the application of tasteless modern paint schemes. In an Hodgson Fowler church, the application of paint to what were meant to be exposed stone surfaces, as in arcades and windows, is especially inappropriate. It is something against which he fulminated, and about which he may well have used one of his favourite epithets – hideous! What little remains of Fowler's decorative schemes now badly needs to be preserved before all is lost.

There are less tangible characteristics of Hodgson Fowler's work. Forty or so years ago, when the earlier phases of the Gothic Revival were beginning to be re-assessed and freshly appreciated, building of Fowler's style and period was very unfashionable, even despised. His work was thought of at best as unremarkable. Peter Anson, in his work on church furnishings, says that his work, along with that of his contemporaries, 'can only be described as dull.'[2] An equally inappropriate assessment is given of the church at Ravensthorpe in Pevsner's West Riding volume. It is only mentioned in the addenda to the 2nd edition, and even then this remarkably dignified incomplete church is dismissed as, 'not of great interest, but commodious.'[3] It can only be wondered whether the author of such words had even seen the church. Other significant work by Fowler is completely omitted from the same volume; e.g. St. Hilda's Halifax and the church at Scotton near Knaresborough, which is included in Betjeman's Collins Guide.

Hopefully we can now begin to appreciate more fully the subtleties of late Victorian and Edwardian church architecture, for much of it is of a very high standard. Unlike the sometimes bizarre creations of earlier architects, Fowler's work has only the occasional idiosyncratic oddity – the squinches at the west end of Revesby, the internal arches supporting the towers at Bearpark and Upper Poppleton, the wooden platform under the bell turret at Beadlam. At its best, it is impressive, with a quiet dignity. Indeed, Pevsner's description of All Saints, Lincoln, as, 'nothing spectacular, but dignified,'[4] could be applied to much of his work. Where the money was available, he produced work of gentle good taste and high quality in design and workmanship, and he had an unerring eye for proportion and pleasing composition.

Hodgson Fowler's churches have one focus – the altar on its steps at the east end. This applies whether or not a chancel screen is part of the design. There is a piece of folklore in the diocese of Durham that Fowler was opposed to chancel screens. That cannot be true, for they were integral to the design of many of his smaller churches. Larger churches were usually designed without them, but St. Faith's Lincoln is an obvious exception. Where they have been introduced later, they sometimes detract from the integrity of the building, and it could be hoped that the folksy examples at Tow Law and New Holland might one day be removed. It could be speculated that even the splendid example at Marsden might have been better omitted, and a rood beam and figures, as at All Saints Lincoln substituted.

CHAPTER SIX
C. Hodgson Fowler, the Churchman

With or without chancel screens, Hodgson Fowler's churches have a great sense of liturgical purpose. They are, above all else, settings for the Church's worship, and especially the celebration of the Eucharist. They are most definitely the work of a churchman, and an English churchman at that. Although he was the first male member of his family for three generations not to be ordained, Fowler was as deeply a committed son of the Church of England as were his clerical brother and ancestors. He was as deeply involved in its life as it was possible to be.

Although he did work on secular buildings, where he is remembered, it is quite rightly as a church architect. A good many of his non-church commissions also had ecclesiastical connections, as in the design of schools, parsonages and church institutes.

Fowler's obituary in the *Durham County Advertiser* demonstrates how deeply involved he was as a layman in the life and politics of the Church he loved. It mentions that he was a member of the House of Laymen of the Province of York, that he had a seat on the Durham Diocesan Conference, and was a steward of the Durham Diocesan Sons of the Clergy Society. It also records that on 26th November 1910, less than three weeks before his death, he took a leading part in the deliberations of the local Ruri-decanal Conference.[1]

In the bottom right hand corner of his memorial window in St. Oswald's church, Durham, Hodgson Fowler is shown dressed in what looks like a cassock, kneeling at a faldstool and presenting a church plan before a large crucifix, whilst Durham Cathedral can be seen through a two light Perpendicular window behind him. The inscription speaks of him as, '... for 30 years a constant worshipper at the Altar of this church.' Mrs. Fowler probably chose those words carefully, for he was a worshipper, 'at the Altar,' and not just, 'in this church.' It seems that Grace Fowler shared her husband's High Church convictions, for her gravestone records that she was a member of the Third Order of one of the newly-revived Anglican sisterhoods.

His writings show Hodgson Fowler's theology and churchmanship, but his churches demonstrate it even more eloquently. He was a man of his time – an Anglican greatly influenced by the second phase of the Tractarian movement. In the first phase the Church of England had rediscovered its Catholic identity and its unbroken links with the pre-Reformation Church of this land. In its second, 'ritualist,' phase, it began to apply this identity to

Charles Hodgson Fowler, as portrayed in the memorial window in St Oswald's Church, Durham

its worship. The Mass was slowly beginning to regain its place as the central act of the Church's life. This was expressed in its new buildings, and, not least, in those of Charles Hodgson Fowler.

Having been taken ill whilst working at Rochester Cathedral early in December 1910, Fowler returned home to Durham, but in the early hours of Wednesday, 14th December, he suffered a fatal stroke. Both the respect in which Fowler was held by the Church and his churchmanship are reflected in the details of his funeral service, held in Durham Cathedral on Saturday 17th December 1910, and reported at length in the *Durham County Advertiser*. His body was carried into the Cathedral through the south door of the cloister. It was received by the Bishop of Jarrow, six members of the Cathedral Chapter and a Minor Canon. The music included works by Dykes, Felton and Barnby, and the hymns sung were, 'Jesus lives!' and, 'Now the labourer's task is o'er.' The most telling and unusual feature of the service was that the Holy Communion was celebrated, something which hints of 'advanced' churchmanship even today, let alone in Durham Cathedral in 1910. We are told that the body was enclosed in an unpolished oak coffin of old English design with a cross of white wood running the full length of the lid. It was covered by a pall of corded violet silk with a richly embroidered fringe and a cross of white silk running the full length.

The body was taken by the 10.29 a.m. express train from Durham, and, after another short service at Nettleham church, was buried in the churchyard extension on the opposite side of the village street, on the afternoon of the same day. An almost equally impressive list of worthies is recorded as being present at Nettleham as were at Durham.[2]

We do not understand Hodgson Fowler's churches unless we understand his motivation in designing them. This motivation is eloquently illustrated, in his own words, in his reaction to the work of another architect of similar principles. In his paper on Nottinghamshire Churches, Fowler recounts how he walked unprepared into the church at Plumtree, recently restored by G.F. Bodley:

It was if I had been carried back to the days before the faith was well nigh lost and love waxed cold, the days when churches were really used and were the true homes of the people, and when God's altar was the point from which and around which all the beauties of the building centered (sic.) All this I found in Plumtree Church; the stately solemn nave with walls and roof all warm with rich yet quiet colour, the low dark open seats, the rood screen, its carving and its fretwork richly gilt, while seen beyond and through it was one of the most beautiful windows of modern days, bright with the figures of saint and angel, and, as its centre, the effigy of Him in whose honour all this beauty had been lavished.'[3]

Such was the vision which motivated Charles Hodgson Fowler in his designing of new churches.

CHAPTER SEVEN
In Conclusion

Charles Hodgson Fowler was responsible for a vast amount of architectural work. The author has a card index of over 250 buildings which Fowler built, rebuilt, restored, furnished, or to which he made additions. That list could be substantially increased by methodical research. And yet he is now virtually unknown.

Even in gatherings in which some knowledge of ecclesiology might reasonably be expected, the mention of Fowler's name may bring no response or a polite enquiry beginning with, "Who ...'. In Lincolnshire, his final resting place, and a county with a very large body of his work, the name Fowler is invariably linked with James Fowler of Louth. Paradoxically Fowler of Louth is better known and better documented than Hodgson Fowler, even though James Fowler's work is less widespread numerically and geographically, and is inferior in quality. The latter contentious point may be demonstrated by comparing the churches of two neighbouring parishes in Lincoln – All Saints and St. Swithin's. The former is one of Hodgson Fowler's most dignified and beautiful buildings, whilst the latter, by James Fowler, is a vast rock-faced barn which displays neither originality, nor subtlety, nor piety.

At least four reasons could be proposed for Hodgson Fowler's current obscurity.

First, he practised in Durham and not in London. Had his first professional post not been as Clerk of the Works at Durham Cathedral, and had he set up in practice in London rather than in the North East, the quality of his work would surely have brought him more fashionable and well funded commissions over a wider area. Furthermore in our contemporary culture, which London dominates more than in the 19th century, we tend to treat anything not emanating from the metropolis as necessarily of the second order.

Secondly, because Fowler practised in the North East, the overwhelming majority of his work is restricted to the four counties in which he had connections – Co. Durham, Yorkshire, Lincolnshire, and Nottinghamshire. He can therefore be dismissed as an architect of only regional significance, and yet that does not account for his neglect even in those four counties.

Thirdly, Hodgson Fowler's work is of a currently unfashionable style and date. As argued above, although the more brash and exciting work

59

of the earlier architects of the Gothic Revival is now appreciated or admired, the late Victorian and Edwardian is still often disregarded. Surely the time is now ripe for a revived appreciation of the quieter quality of some of the work from this later period.

Fourthly, Hodgson Fowler was first and foremost a church architect. In an increasingly secular culture, ignorance of ecclesiastical art and architecture is understandably becoming increasingly the norm, even amongst those who would consider themselves to be aesthetically and culturally aware. Ecclesiology is now the strange and obscure interest of a tiny minority. This fact is no excuse for ignorance on the part of those who have the care of church buildings.

At his best, Hodgson Fowler produced good and distinctive buildings. They have a feeling of unostentatious dignity and fitness for their purpose, which is often not equalled by the work of other architects. Of course there were comparative failures. Some have pointed to the less than satisfactory rebuilding at Sowerby in Yorkshire and at South Ferriby in Lincolnshire. Amongst his new churches, it might be argued that St. Peter's Woodhall Spa is less than inspiring, although part of the problem there is the furnishings of later designers. Some of the early work is also below par when compared with what was to come. But, in churches like St. Ignatius Hendon, St. Columba's Southwick, St. Bartholomew's Marsden, St. Peter's Norton, and St. Faith's and All Saints Lincoln, Fowler produced work which stands comparison with virtually anything by his contemporaries, with the exception of Bodley and Garner.

Although his early work has a feel strangely behind the times, Hodgson Fowler's mature designs can be argued, in some ways, to point to what is to come later. From the 1880s onwards he used late Gothic styles in a free and unfussy way, which paves the way for the work of Temple Moor and W.H. Brierley, and which prefigures the Gothic minimalism of some churches built after the First World War. One small, but very important, group of his churches – the basilicas – were ground breaking. St. Columba's Southwick is 30 years ahead of its time, and these churches point the way to the Romanesque churches designed by a number of architects in the 1930s.

In his time Hodgson Fowler's name was well known and his work was well respected. His abilities were highly rated by the great professional names of his youth, and his potential was recognised in his appointment as Clerk of the Works at Durham at the young age of 24. His enormous reputation later in life is shown by the number of prestigious appointments he held. It is high time his work was rescued from obscurity and restored to the recognition it deserves.

It is fitting to end with the tribute paid to Charles Hodgson Fowler by the Bishop of Jarrow in Durham Cathedral on Sunday, 18th December 1910, the day after his funeral:

> Gifted with genius and an adequate knowledge of his task, he brought to his profession high ideals and a spirit of real devotion. The unostentatious yet noble simplicity of his Christian faith is reflected again and again in the beautiful churches which he built. Of deep religious convictions himself, he impressed others by the reality of his life and the earnestness of his purpose. ... He loved his art for itself alone, and he dedicated his gifts to the Giver who had bestowed them. We shall miss his familiar figure in this place, but he cannot be forgotten. Here in this Cathedral, in this county, and in many another spot, of him, as of another craftsman, we can say, '*Si monumentum requiris, circumspice!*'[1]

The entrance to the south chapel, St Bartholomew's, Marsden

APPENDIX 1

The New Churches and Chapels of C. Hodgson Fowler

This list will almost certainly be incomplete.

The buildings marked with a double asterisk (**) are, in the subjective opinion of the present writer, the most interesting or outstanding.

1. Barton-upon-Humber, St. Chad, Lincs. 1902. (now demolished)

2. Beadlam, St. Hilda, Yorks., 1882.

3. Bearpark, St. Edmund, Co. Durham, 1877.

4. Belvedere, St. Augustine, Gilbert Road, Kent, 1911

5. **Bishopthorpe, St. Andrew, Yorks., 1898–1902.

6. **Bournemouth, St. Ambrose, West Cliff Road, Dorset, 1898–1907.

7. Bracebridge Heath, St. John the Evangelist, Lincs., 1908.

8. Broom, St. Katherine's Chapel, Co. Durham, 1881. (now a private dwelling)

9. **Carlton Minniott, St. Lawrence, Yorks., 1896.

10. **Cheltenham, St. Paul's College Chapel, Glos.,1909.

11. **Cleethorpes, St. Aidan, Lincs., 1905.

12. **Crosland Moor, St. Barnabas, Park Road, Huddersfield, Yorks., 1902.

13. ** Dawdon, Ss. Hild and Helen, Mount Stewart Street, Seaham, Co. Durham, 1910.

14. Easington, All Saints, Yorks. 1888.

15. East Rainton, St. Cuthbert, Co. Durham, 1866.

16. Faldingworth, All Saints, Lincs. 1890.

17. Flixborough, All Saints, Lincs., 1888.

18. **Great Habton, St. Chad, Yorks., 1884.

19. **Grove, St. Helen, Nottinghamshire, 1882.

20. Halifax, St. Hilda, Yorks., 1902.

21. Hampsthwaite, St. Thomas Becket, Yorks., 1902.

22. Harrogate, Chapel of Woodard Girls' School, Yorks.

23. Hartlepool, Fisherman's Church, Co. Durham, 1886. (now demolished)

24. **Hartlepool, St. Paul, Co. Durham, 1885.

25. Harton (South Shields), St. Peter, Co. Durham, 1866.

26. Haswell, St. Paul, Co. Durham, 1865.

27. **Hebburn, St. Oswald, Co. Durham, 1882–90.

28. Hedworth, St. Nicholas, Boldon Colliery, Co. Durham, 1882.

29. Hepple, Christ Church, Northumberland, 1893.

30. Hetton-le-Hole, Moorsley Mission Chapel, Co. Durham, 1881.

31. High Hoyland, All Hallows, Yorks., 1904. (now used as an art studio)

32. Houghton-le-Spring, Cemetery Chapel, Co. Durham, 1874.

33. Houghton-le-Spring, Mission Chapel, Co. Durham, 1882.

34. Howden-le-Wear (or Fir Tree), St. Mary, Co. Durham, 1864.

35. **Kensington, St. Columb, Lancaster Road, Notting Hill, London, 1900. (now St. Sava's Serbian Church)

36. **Leadgate, St. Ives, Co. Durham, 1865–79.

37. **Lincoln, All Saints, Monks Road, 1904.

38. **Lincoln, St. Faith, Charles Street West, 1895.

39. **Marsden, St. Bartholomew, Yorks., 1895.

40. Mexborough, All Saints, Denaby Main, Yorks., 1899. (demolished in 1970s)

41. Middlesbrough, St. Barnabas, Linthorpe, Yorks., 1888.

42. Middleton-in-Teesdale, St. Mary, Co. Durham, 1878.

43. Murton, Holy Trinity, Co. Durham, 1876.

44. New Holland, Christ Church, Lincs., 1897.

45. **Norton, St. Peter, Yorks., 1889-1913.

46. **Ordsall, St. Alban, London Road, Retford, Notts. 1901. (now being converted into an arts centre.)

47. **Ravensthorpe, St. Saviour, Yorks. 1901.

48. **Revesby, St. Lawrence, Lincs. 1889.

49. Romanby, St. James, Northallerton, Yorks., 1882.

50. Scotton, St. Thomas the Apostle, Yorks., 1889.

51. **Spennymoor, St. Andrew, Tudhoe Grange, Co. Durham, 1884.

52. Stourton (Leeds), St. Andrew, Yorks., 1898. (demolished 1973.)

53. **Sunderland, St. Aidan, Ryhope Road, Grangetown, Co. Durham, 1910

54. **Sunderland, St. Columba, Cornhill Road, Southwick, Co. Durham, 1888.

55. **Sunderland, St. Ignatius the Martyr, Suffolk Street, Hendon, Co. Durham, 1889.

56. Sunderland, St. Mary, South Hylton, Co. Durham. 1880.

57. Sykehouse, Holy Trinity, Yorks. 1869.

58. **Thurlstone, St. Saviour, Yorks. 1905.

59. Toft-next-Newton, Ss. Peter and Paul, Lincs. 1889. (now a private dwelling)

60. **Tow Law, Ss. Philip and James, Co. Durham, 1869.

61. Trimdon Station, St. Paul, Deaf Hill, Co. Durham, 1882.

62. Upper Poppleton, All Saints, Yorks., 1891.

63. West Harton (South Shields), All Saints, Co. Durham, 1887.

64. Woodhall Spa, St. Peter, Lincs., 1893.

APPENDIX 2

A Selected List of 40 Churches with Works of Rebuilding, Addition or Restoration by C. Hodgson Fowler.

This selection is arbitrary, and there are many other churches, with work by Hodgson Fowler, which are well worth inspection.

1. Alfreton, St. Martin, Derbys.

2. Barkston, St. Nicholas, Lincs.

3. Birdsall, St. Mary, Yorks.

4. Bishop Auckland, Bishop's Palace Chapel, Co. Durham.

5. Copmanthorpe, St. Giles, Yorks.

6. Coton, St. Peter, Cambridgeshire.

7. Cranwell, St. Andrew, Lincs.

8. Drax, Ss. Peter and Paul, Yorks.

9. Durham Cathedral.

10. Durham, St. Margaret of Antioch.

11. Flamborough, St. Oswald, Yorks.

12. Fridaythorpe, St. Mary, Yorks.

13. Greetham, All Saints, Lincs.

14. Hameringham, All Saints, Lincs.

15. Kirby Misperton, St. Laurence, Yorks.

16. Kirk Hammerton, St. John, Yorks.

17. Kirton-in-Holland, Ss. Peter and Paul, Lincs.

18. Lincoln, St. Peter at Gowts.

19. Maplebeck, St. Radegund, Notts.

20. Northallerton, All Saints, Yorks.

21. Rochester Cathedral.

22. Rolleston, Holy Trinity, Notts.

23. Ryther, All Saints, Yorks.

24. Salton, St. John of Beverley, Yorks.

25. Scawton, St. Mary, Yorks.

26. Sellatyn, St. Mary, Shropshire.

27. Sherburn, St. Hilda, Yorks.

28. Shildon, St. John, Co. Durham.

29. Sinnington, All Saints, Yorks.

30. South Ferriby, St. Nicholas, Lincs.

31. South Kyme, St. Mary and All Saints, Lincs.

32. Stillingflett, St. Helen, Yorks.

33. Stowell, St. Leonard, Gloucestershire.

34. Sturton-le-Steeple, Ss. Peter and Paul, Notts.

35. Thorganby, All Saints, Lincs.

36. Wanlip, Our Lady and St. Nicholas, Leicestershire.

37. Wetwang, St. Nicholas, Yorks.

38. Winterton, All Saints, Lincs.

39. Witton-le-Wear, Ss. Philip and James, Co. Durham.

40. York, Holy Trinity, Micklegate.

END-NOTES

Chapter 1

1 J.A. Venn, *Alumni Cantabrigiensis, 1751–1900*, Cambridge, 1944 p.552.
2 J. Foster, *Alumni Oxoniensis, 1715–1886*, Oxford, 1887, p.486.
3 Venn, *Alumni Cantabrigiensis*, p.554.
4 J. Jamieson, *Durham at the Opening of the Twentieth Century: Contemporary Biographies*, ed. W.R. Pike, Brighton, 1906, p.215.
5 David Cole, *The Work of Sir Gilbert Scott*, London, 1980, p.232ff.
6 Cole, p.86.
7 Cole, p.69ff.
8 Cole, p.82ff.
9 R.I.B.A. Drawings Catalogue.
10 Royal Academy of Arts, List of Exhibitors, p.149.
11 R.I.B.A. Nomination Papers.
12 Charles Hadfield, *The Canals of the East Midlands*, 2nd edition, Newton Abbot, 1970, p.238.

Chapter 2

1 Durham Chapter Acts, 1864.
2 See N.Pevsner, *The Buildings of England: Durham*, 2nd edition, revised by E. Williamson, London, 1983; and Durham County Record Office, Hodgson Fowler Drawings Collection (D/HF).
3 Pevsner, p.475.
4 Pevsner, p.476 et al.
5 Tyne and Wear Archives, Wood & Oakley Collection, DT/WO/1/1 and DT/WO/1/2.
6 Tyne and Wear Archives, DT/WO/1/1.
7 Pevsner, p.167.
8 For all Hodgson Fowler work at Durham Cathedral, see Durham Dean and Chapter Muniments HLB Drawings Collection, kept by Durham University Library at 5 The College, Durham.
9 C. Hodgson Fowler, 'Church Restoration: What to do, and what to avoid,' in *Associated Architectural Societies Reports and Papers* Vol.XVII (1883), p.14.
10 *Archaeologia*, Vol.XLV, pp.383–404.
11 Pevsner, p.167.

12 See Durham C.R.O. D/HF.
13 Obituary in *Durham County Advertiser*, 16th December 1910.
14 R.I.B.A. Nomination Papers.
15 J. Jamieson, Op Cit., p.215.
16 The restoration of Mavis Enderby church in 1875.
17 Lincolnshire Archives, Fowler Plans 64.
18 Obituary in *The Builder*, 24th Dec. 1910, pp.794–5.
19 Tyne and Wear Archives DT/WO/1/95.
20 *Durham County Advertiser*, 16th Dec. 1910.
21 *Durham County Advertiser*, 16th Dec. 1910.
22 Obituary in *Building News*, No.2919, 16th Dec. 1910.
23 Obituary in *R.I.B.A. Journal*, 24th Dec. 1910, p.142.
24 *Transactions of the Archaeological and Architectural Society of Durham and Northumberland* Vol.I, p.xlix.
25 As above, Vol.II. p.xlii and p. 271.
26 *Yorkshire Archaeological Journal* Vol. 9 (1886) p.395.
27 *Newark Advertiser*, 7th June 1911.
28 *Associated Architectural Societies Reports and Papers* Vol.XIV (1877) p.57 and p.73.
29 *Associated Societies Reports etc.* Vol.XV (1880), p.219 and p.131.
30 See above at 9.
31 See above at 10.
32 Tyne and Wear Archives DT/WO/1.

Chapter 3

1 *Associated Societies Reports etc.* Vol.XVII (1883), pp.9–21.
2 Rev. John Ford (ed.), *The Town on the Street*, Sturton-le-Steeple, 1975, p.74.
3 Fowler, 'Church Restoration,' p.12.
4 Fowler, p.9.
5 Fowler, p.15.
6 Fowler, p.18.
7 Fowler, p.19.
8 Unpublished B.A. dissertation by Christobel Jane Hatcher, 'Principles of Restoration, as exemplified in the work of Charles Hodgson Fowler, 1840–1910, Architect and Ecclesiologist, in some Yorkshire Churches,' 1972, in Architecture Dept. Resource Centre at University of Newcastle-upon-Tyne.

9   N.Pevsner, *The Buildings of England: Yorkshire, the North Riding*, London, 1966, p.334.

10   See above in Chapter 2 at 27 and 28.

11   Pevsner, *North Riding*, p.290.

12   N. Pevsner & J. Harris, *The Buildings of England: Lincolnshire*, 2nd edition revised by N. Antram, London, 1989, p.360.

13   Pevsner & Harris, p.665.

14   J.C. Cox, *Lincolnshire*, Little Guide Series, London, 1916.

15   Pevsner, *Durham*, p.46.

16   Fowler, 'Church Restoration,' p.20.

17   Fowler, p.12.

18   C. Hodgson Fowler, 'Some Account of Salton Church, Yorkshire,' in *Associated Architectural Societies Reports and Papers*, Vol.XV(1880), p.219.

19   Fowler, 'Church Restoration,' p.21.

Chapter 4

1   C. Hodgson Fowler, 'Some Characteristics of Nottinghamshire Churches,' in *Associated Architectural Societies Reports and Papers* Vol.XV(1880), p.139.

2   Pevsner, *Durham*, p.312.

3   Fowler, 'Nottinghamshire Churches,' p.131.

4   Fowler, p.134.

5   Fowler, p.135.

6   Fowler, p.135.

7   Henry Thorold, *Lincolnshire Churches Revisited*, Salisbury, 1989, p.154.

8   Fowler, 'Church Restoration,' p.16.

9   Tyne and Wear Archives DT/WO/1/46 p.11.

10   C. Hodgson Fowler, 'Glentworth Church,' in *Associated Architectural Societies Reports and Papers* Vol.XIV(1877) p.58.

11   Drawings held by the Parochial Church Council in the church.

12   Tyne and Wear Archives DT/WO/1/94 p.22.

13   Fowler, 'Nottinghamshire Churches,' p.140.

Chapter 5

1   Lincolnshire Archives, Fowler Plans 50.

2   Peter F.Anson, *Fashions in Church Furnishings 1840–1940*, 2nd edition, London, 1965, p.271.

3   N.Pevsner, *The Buildings of England: Yorkshire, the West Riding*, 2nd edition revised by E. Ratcliffe, London, 1967, p.644.

4   Pevsner, *Lincolnshire*, p.496.

Chapter 6

1   *Durham County Advertiser*, 16th Dec. 1910.

2   *Durham County Advertiser*, 23rd Dec. 1910.

3   Fowler, 'Nottinghamshire Churches,' p.140.

Chapter 7

1   *Durham County Advertiser*, 23rd Dec. 1910.

BIBLIOGRAPHY

The place of publication is London unless otherwise stated.

P.F. Anson   *Fashions in Church Furnishings 1840–1940*, 2nd edition, 1965.

B.F.L. Clarke   *Church Builders of the Nineteenth Century*, 1969.

D. Cole   *The Work of Sir Gilbert Scott*, 1980.

J.C. Cox   *Lincolnshire*, in the Little Guide Series, 1916.

J. Ford (ed.)   *The Town on the Street*, Sturton-le-Steeple, 1975.

J. Foster   *Alumni Oxoniensis, 1715–1886*, Oxford, 1887.

C. Hadfield   *The Canals of the East Midlands*, 2nd edition, Newton Abbot, 1970

J. Jamieson   *Durham at the Opening of the Twentieth Century: Contemporary Biographies*, ed. T.W.Pike, Brighton, 1906.

N. Pevsner   *The Buildings of England: Cheshire*, 1971.

N. Pevsner   *The Buildings of England: Durham*, 2nd edition revised by E. Williamson, 1983.

N. Pevsner   *The Buildings of England: Leicestershire and Rutland*, 2nd edition revised Williamson & Brandwood, 1984.

N. Pevsner   *The Buildings of England: Nottinghamshire*, 2nd edition revised by E. Williamson, 1979.

N. Pevsner   *The Buildings of England: Shropshire*, 1958.

N. Pevsner   *The Buildings of England: Yorkshire*, the North Riding, 1966.

N. Pevsner   *The Buildings of England: Yorkshire, the West Riding,*
                           2nd edition revised by E. Ratcliffe, 1967.

N. Pevsner and   *The Buildings of England: London 3, North West,* 1991.
B. Cherry

N. Pevsner and   *The Buildings of England: Lincolnshire,* 2nd edition
J. Harris   revised by N. Antram, 1989.

N. Pevsner and   *The Buildings of England: Hampshire and the Isle of*
D. Lloyd   *Wight,* 1967.

N. Pevsner and   *The Buildings of England: York and the East Riding,*
D. Neave   1995.

N. Pevsner and   *The Buildings of England: West Kent and the Weald,*
J. Newman   1980.

N. Pevsner and   *The Buildings of England: Northumberland,* 1992.
I. Richmond

N. Pevsner and   *The Buildings of England: Gloucestershire, the Cotswolds,*
D. Verey   1979.

N. Pevsner and   *The Buildings of England: Gloucestershire, the Vale and*
D. Verey   *the Forest of Dean,* 1976.

H. Thorold   *Lincolnshire Churches Revisited,* Salisbury, 1989.

J.A. Venn   *Alumni Cantabrigiensis, 1751–1900,* Cambridge, 1944.

D. Ware   *Short Dictionary of British Architects,* 1967.

Journals and Proceedings

Archaeologia Vol. XLV.

Archaeologia Aeliana: New Series Vol. VII (1876).

Associated Architectural Societies Reports and Papers, Vol.XIV (1877), Vol.XV (1880), Vol.XVII (1883).

R.I.B.A. Journal, 24th Dec. 1910.

Transactions of the Archaeological and Architectural Society of Durham and Northumberland Vol.I (1862–8), Vol.II (1869–79), Vol.V (1896–1905), Vol.VI (1906–11).

Yorkshire Archaeological Journal Vol.IX (1886), Vol.XX (1909), Vol. XXI (1911).

Published Papers by C. Hodgson Fowler

'Church Restoration: What to do, and what to avoid,' in *Associated Architectural Societies Reports and Papers* Vol.XVII (1883).

'Glentworth Church,' in Associated Architectural Societies' Reports and Papers Vol.XIV (1877).

'Some Characteristics of Nottinghamshire Churches,' in *Associated Architectural Societies Reports and Papers* Vol.XV (1880).

'Some Account of Salton Church, Yorkshire,' in *Associated Architectural Societies' Reports and Papers* Vol.XV (1880).

'Stillingfleet Church,' in *Associated Architectural Societies' Reports and Papers* Vol. XIV (1877).

Newspapers and Periodicals

Building News No.2919, 16th Dec. 1910.

The Builder, 24th Dec. 1910.

The Durham County Advertiser, 16th Dec. 1910, and 23rd Dec. 1910.

The Newark Advertiser, 7th June 1911.

The Times, 15th Dec. 1910

Archive Sources

Durham Chapter Acts

Durham County Record Office, Hodgson Fowler Drawings Collection, Ref. D/HF

Durham Dean and Chapter Muniments, HLB Drawings Collection, 5 The College, Durham

Lincolnshire Archives, Fowler Plans

Royal Academy of Arts, List of Exhibitors

R.I.B.A. Biographical File on C. Hodgson Fowler.

R.I.B.A. Drawings Catalogue.

R.I.B.A. Nomination Papers.

Tyne and Wear Archives, Wood and Oakley Collection, Ref. DT/WO/1/1-95.

Unpublished Dissertation

C.J.Hatcher, 'Principles of Restoration, as exemplified in the work of Charles Hodgson Fowler, 1840-1910, Architect and Ecclesiologist, in some Yorkshire Churches,' 1972, - in Architecture Department Resources Centre, University of Newcastle-upon-Tyne.

DURHAM COUNTY LOCAL HISTORY SOCIETY

Publications – 1st December 2000

H.T. Dickinson, *Radical Politics in the North-East of England in the Later Eighteenth Century*
(1979) card covers, 24 pp (members 40p) 80p

K. Emsley & C.M. Fraser, The Courts of the County Palatine of Durham (1984)
laminated covers, 112 pp (ISBN 0-902958-07-0) (members £4.50) £7.50

D.S. Reid, *The Durham Crown Lordships* (1990)
laminated covers, 196 pp (ISBN 0-902958-13-5) (members £4.50) £7.50

A.J. Heesom, *Durham City and its M.P.s; 1678-1992* (1992)
laminated covers, 68 pp (ISBN 0-902958-11-9) (members £2.50) £3.50

An Historical Atlas of County Durham (1993)
laminated covers, 88 pp (ISBN 0-902958-14-3) (members £4.00) £6.00

Bulletin Index: Numbers 1-50, June 1964-May 1993 (1994)
laminated covers, 25 pp £1.00

D.J. Butler, *Durham 1849: The 1849 Public Health Report on Durham City* (1997)
laminated covers, 29 pp (ISBN 0-902958-15-1) (members £2.50) £4.00

H.W. Jackson, *A County Durham Man at Trafalgar: Cumby of the Bellerophon* (1997)
coloured laminated covers, 38 pp (ISBN 0-902958-16-X) (members £2.50) £4.00

W.Stokes (ed.), *Memoirs of a Primitive Methodist: Eventide Memories and Recollections by
Henry Green (1855-1932)* (1997)
laminated covers, 43 pp (ISBN 0-902958-17-8) (members £2.50) £4.00

C.M. Newman, *The Bowes of Streatlam, County Durham: The Politics and Religion of a Tudor
Gentry Family* (1999)
laminated covers, 32 pp (ISBN 0-902958-18-6) (members £2.50) £4.00

M. Bush, *Durham and the Pilgrimage of Grace* (2000)
laminated covers, 68 pp (ISBN 0-902958-19-4) (members £2.50) £4.00

G.R. Batho (ed.), *Durham Biographies,* volume 1 (2000)
laminated covers, 156 pp (ISBN 0-902958-20-8) (members £4.00) £5.00

G.R. Batho (ed.), *Durham Biographies,* volume 2 (2002)
laminated covers, 156 pp (ISBN 0-902958-22-4) (members £4.00) £5.00

Documentary Series

4. H.J. Smith, *A Mirthless Mirrour Mischievously Managed: The Dispute over the Living of
Middleton-in-Teesdale. 1661* (1980)
card covers, 14 pp (ISBN 0-902958-05-4) 50p

Titles can be ordered from:
Professor G.R. Batho
The Miners' Hall
Red Hill
DURHAM
DH1 4BB

Cheques payable to Durham County Local History Society (include 70p for post & packing)